Prayers That Avail Much®

for Singles

James 5:16

by
Germaine Copeland
Word Ministries, Inc.

And this is the confidence that we have in him, that, if we ask any thing according to his will, he heareth us: and if we know that he hear us, whatsoever we ask, we know that we have the petitions that we desired of him.

1 John 5:14,15

Harrison House
Tulsa, Oklahoma

07 06 05 04   10 9 8 7 6 5 4 3 2 1

Prayers That Avail Much® *for Singles*
ISBN 1-57794-583-2
Copyright © 2004 by Germaine Copeland
38 Sloan St.
Roswell, Georgia 30075

Published by Harrison House, Inc.
P. O. Box 35035
Tulsa, Oklahoma 74153

CONTENTS

Introduction

Several years ago a certain singles ministry compiled a list of prayer needs that was representative of many single people's needs today, and at last a book has been written to provide the prayers to meet those needs. The people in that ministry had prayed from the other *Prayers That Avail Much*® family books with wonderful results, and they knew the power of praying the Word of God. They, along with a multitude of other believers, have proven that this method of praying is effective, and that it does avail much (James 5:16)!

The prayers in this book will give you a spiritual focal point. The Lord Jesus Christ is sovereign; He is your role model. As His representative here on earth determine your identity, your integrity, and your influence. In *Living Every Single Moment* Angela Payne writes, "We don't need to be blinded by our emotions, tears, joys, possibilities, goose bumps, chill bumps, or glow-in-the-dark feelings. It must be on Him alone that our trust is established. He directs our steps and hearts and withholds no good thing from us."[1]

Jesus understands you and your situation. He was tempted in all points, even as you are, yet He was without sin (Heb. 4:15). He walked the earth as a single man.

---

[1] Angela Payne, *Living Every Single Moment* (Birmingham, AL: New Hope Publishers, 2000), page 26.

Whether you are believing for a spouse, single by choice, divorced, or widowed, you are complete in Him (Col. 2:10). You are a child of the Most High God. He chose you before the foundation of the world to be His very own (Eph. 1:4).

First Corinthians 7:32 is a Scripture we seldom hear: "One who is unmarried is concerned about the things of the Lord, how he may please the Lord" (NAS). Single people have sometimes questioned me when I have quoted this verse, but even if it isn't what we want to hear, it is still written in the Bible. If you determine your identification, integrity, and influence according to the Word while you are single, you will stay centered on the things of God. You are a valuable asset in the Kingdom when your goal is to speak the truth in love and grow up into Christ in all things. Avoid becoming obsessed with finding a mate; instead, focus your attention on developing your relationship with your heavenly Father. With His help, you can be a world-changer!

Establish a time to be alone with God and to fellowship with Him. The prayers in this book will bring spiritual growth, emotional healing, and a greater intimacy with the Father. As you pray, you will be strengthened, enlightened, and encouraged. Prayer is imperative. Jesus said, "Watch and pray that you may not enter into temptation" (Mark 14:38 ESV). May these prayers help you fulfill your destiny as you obey His command, and you will find fulfillment in your life as a single person.

A Word to the Single

You were created with a need to love and be loved. Everyone desires intimacy. Everyone wants his or her life to be significant. Too often this need is interpreted as a desire to be married and is based on the assumption that another human being will fulfill this desire. The only source of this need for intimacy is God Himself, Who may meet the need through another person. However, our focus must be on the One Who made us, Who knows us, and Who understands us.

Often it is after many failed relationships or marriages that a person discovers that there is no human being who can fulfill this God-given desire. When an individual becomes absorbed with the idea of marriage, it is easy to cross the line into obsessive-compulsive behavior. This creates a barrier, often driving people away rather than drawing them closer. This opens the door for distrust, leading to a suspicion that God is withholding good things, when He has promised in His Word not to withhold any good thing from those who walk uprightly (Ps. 84:11).

The effectual, fervent prayers of a righteous person avail much (James 5:16). God defined the person whose prayers are answered: a righteous person—a person in right standing with God. Someone has defined *righteousness* as "doing it God's way and risking the consequences."

So often it seems that there is a fear of living His way. "Doing it God's way" demands trust in the One Who has your best interest at heart.

You may be tired of hearing, "Seek first the kingdom of God and His righteousness" (Matt. 6:33 NKJV). Children of God are citizens of this Kingdom now in this lifetime. Jesus said, "The Kingdom of God is within you" (Luke 17:21). To truly seek God, "His way of doing and being right" (Matt. 6:33 AMP), may require you to accept personal singleness. Is this easy? Probably not! *But* God is faithful. He will not fail you; He will help you.

In her book *Living Every Single Moment*, Angela Payne wrote, "I have noted that women may have vast personality differences, diverse cultural backgrounds, and different languages, but we also have a common thread of emotions that is intricately interwoven in our hearts and spirit."[2]

Women relate to one another—whether single or married. However, this book is not written "for women only," but also for single males who will likewise benefit from these scriptural prayers.

Avoid becoming compulsive and obsessive about finding a mate. Obsessive-compulsive behavior leads to manipulation and control. Rest in the Lord, stay calm and watchful, exercise self-control, and keep alert, because your

---

[2] Angela Payne, *Living Every Single Moment* (Birmingham, AL: New Hope Publishers, 2000), Preface.

adversary is prowling around seeking whom he may destroy (1 Pet. 5:8). Cast all your anxieties and worries over onto the Lord, because He cares for you (v. 7).

God has a plan for you. He knows what it takes to bring each one of His children to spiritual maturity, and He has spoken in His love letter to you: "I know the thoughts that I think toward you, saith the Lord, thoughts of peace, and not of evil, to give you an expected end" (Jer. 29:11).

It is my prayer that you will trust in the Lord with all your heart and lean not unto your own understanding. In all your ways acknowledge Him, and He will direct your ways (Prov. 3:5,6).

Sincerely in His love,
Germaine Copeland
President and Founder
Word Ministries, Inc.

How To Pray
Prayers That Avail Much®

The prayers in this book are to be used by you for
yourself and for others. They are a matter of the heart.
Deliberately pray and meditate on each prayer. Allow the
Holy Spirit to make the Word of God a reality in your
heart. Your spirit will become alive to God's Word, and
you will begin to think like God thinks and talk like He
talks. You will find yourself poring over His Word,
hungering for more and more. The Father rewards those
who diligently seek Him (Heb. 11:6).

Research and contemplate the spiritual significance of
each verse listed with the prayers. These are by no means the
only Scriptures on certain subjects, but they are a beginning.

These prayers and the study of His Word will transform
your mind and lifestyle. Then others will know that it is
possible to change, and you will give hope to those who come
to you seeking advice. When you admonish someone with the
Word, you are offering spiritual guidance and consolation.

Walk in God's counsel, and prize His wisdom (Ps. 1:1-
3,6; Prov. 4:7,8). People are looking for something on
which they can depend. When others in need come to you,
you can point them to that portion in God's Word that is
the answer to their problem. You will become victorious,

trustworthy, and the one with the answer, for your heart will be fixed and established on His Word (Ps. 112).

Once you begin delving into God's Word, you must commit to ordering your conversation aright (Ps. 50:23). That is being a doer of the Word (James 1:22). Faith always has a good report (Phil. 4:8). You cannot pray effectively for yourself, for someone else, or about something, if you talk negatively about the matter (Matt. 12:34-37). To do so is to be double minded, and a double-minded man can expect to receive *nothing* from God (James 1:6-8).

In Ephesians 4:29-30 AMP it is written:

Let no foul or polluting language, nor evil word nor unwholesome or worthless talk [ever] come out of your mouth, but only such [speech] as is good and beneficial to the spiritual progress of others, as is fitting to the need and the occasion, that it may be a blessing and give grace (God's favor) to those who hear it.

And do not grieve the Holy Spirit of God [do not offend or vex or sadden Him], by Whom you were sealed (marked, branded as God's own, secured) for the day of redemption (of final deliverance through Christ from evil and the consequences of sin).

Reflect on these words and give them time to bring your perspective into line with God's will. Our Father has much, so very much, to say about that little member, the tongue (James 3:5-12). Give the devil no opportunity by getting into worry, unforgiveness, strife, and criticism. Put a stop to idle and foolish talk (Eph. 4:27,31; 5:4). Remember that you are to be a blessing to others (Gal. 6:10).

Talk the answer, not the problem. The answer is in God's Word. To receive that answer, you must have knowledge of the Word—revelation knowledge (1 Cor. 2:7-16). The Holy Spirit, your Teacher, will reveal the things that have been freely given to us by God (John 14:26).

Unite with others in prayer. United prayer is a mighty weapon that the Body of Christ is to use. Jesus said, "When two of you get together on anything at all on earth and make a prayer of it, my Father in heaven goes into action. And when two or three of you are together because of me, you can be sure that I'll be there" (Matt. 18:19,20 THE MESSAGE).

Have faith in God (Mark 11:22), and approach Him confidently (Heb. 4:16 AMP). When you pray according to His will, He hears you. Then you know you have what you ask of Him (1 John 5:14,15 NIV). "Do not throw away your confidence; it will be richly rewarded" (Heb. 10:35 NIV). Allow your spirit to pray by the Holy Spirit. Praise God for the victory now before any manifestation. *Walk by faith and not by sight* (2 Cor. 5:7).

When your faith comes under pressure, don't be moved. As Satan attempts to challenge you, resist him steadfastly in the faith—letting patience have her perfect work (James 1:4). Take the sword of the Spirit and the shield of faith and quench his every fiery dart (Eph. 6:16,17). The entire substitutionary work of Christ was for you. Satan is now a defeated foe, because Jesus conquered him on the cross (Col. 2:14,15). You overcome Satan by the blood of the Lamb and the word of your testimony (Rev. 12:11). "Fight the good fight of faith" (1 Tim. 6:12). Withstand the adversary and "be firm in faith [against his onset—rooted, established, strong, immovable, and determined]" (1 Pet. 5:9 AMP). Speak God's Word boldly and courageously (Eph. 6:19).

Your desire should be to please and to bless the Father. As you pray according to His Word, He joyfully hears that you—His child—are living and walking in the truth (3 John 4).

How exciting to know that the prayers of the saints are forever in the heavenly throne room (Rev. 5:7,8). Hallelujah!

Praise God for His Word and the limitlessness of prayer in the name of Jesus. The privilege of reading and praying the Word in Jesus' name belongs to every child of God. Therefore, run with patience the race that is set before you, looking unto Jesus, the Author and Finisher of your faith (Heb. 12:1,2). God's Word "is able to build you up and to give you [your rightful] inheritance among all God's set-apart ones" (Acts 20:32 AMP).

Commit yourself to pray, and to pray correctly, by approaching the throne of God with your mouth filled with His Word!

Effectual Prayer

...The earnest (heartfelt, continued) prayer of a righteous man makes tremendous power available [dynamic in its working].

James 5:16 AMP

Prayer is fellowshipping with the Father—a vital, personal contact with God, Who is more than enough (Ps. 4:6 MESSAGE). We are to be in constant communion with Him:

For the eyes of the Lord are upon the righteous (those who are upright and in right standing with God,) and His ears are attentive to their prayer....

1 Peter 3:12 AMP

Prayer is not to be a religious form with no power. It is to be effective and accurate and bring *results*. God watches over His Word to perform it (Jer. 1:12 AMP).

Prayer that brings results must be based on God's Word.

For the Word that God speaks is alive and full of power [making it active, operative, energizing, and effective]; it is sharper than any two-edged sword, penetrating to the dividing line of the breath of life (soul) and [the immortal] spirit, and of joints and marrow [of the deepest parts of our nature],

exposing and sifting and analyzing and judging the
very thoughts and purposes of the heart.

Hebrews 4:12 AMP

Prayer is this "living" Word in our mouths. Our
mouths must speak forth faith, for faith is what pleases
God (Heb. 11:6). We hold His Word up to Him in
prayer, and our Father sees Himself in His Word.

God's Word is our contact with Him. We put Him in
remembrance of His Word (Isa. 43:26), asking Him for
what we need in the name of our Lord Jesus. The woman
in Mark 5:25-34 placed a demand on the power of God
when she said, "If I can but touch the hem of his garment,
I will be healed" (v. 28, author's paraphrase). By faith she
touched His clothes and was healed. We remind Him that
He supplies all of our needs according to His riches in
glory by Christ Jesus (Phil. 4:19). That Word does not
return to Him "void [without producing any effect,
useless] but it *shall* accomplish that which I [God] pleases
and purposes], and it shall prosper in the thing for which
I [God] sent it" (Isa. 55:11 AMP). Hallelujah!

God did *not* leave us without His thoughts and His
ways, for we have His Word—which is His bond. God
instructs us to call upon Him, and He will answer and
show us great and mighty things (Jer. 33:3). Prayer is to
be exciting—not drudgery.

It takes someone to pray. God moves as we pray in faith—believing. He says that His eyes run to and fro throughout the whole earth to show Himself strong in behalf of those whose hearts are blameless toward Him (2 Chron. 16:9 AMP). We are blameless in God's sight (Eph. 1:4 AMP). We are His very own children (Eph. 1:5; Gal. 3:26). We are His righteousness in Christ Jesus (2 Cor. 5:21). He tells us to come boldly to the throne of grace and *obtain* mercy and find grace to help in time of need—appropriate and well-timed help (Heb. 4:16 AMP). Praise the Lord!

The prayer armor described in Ephesians 6:11-18 is for every believer, every member of the Body of Christ, who will put it on and walk in it. Second Corinthians 10:4 explains why we need to do that: "for the weapons of our warfare are *not carnal* but mighty through God for the pulling down of [the] strong holds" of the enemy— Satan, the god of this world (2 Cor. 4:4), and all his demonic forces.

There are many different kinds of prayer, such as the prayer of thanksgiving and praise, the prayer of dedication and worship, and the prayer that changes *things* (not God). All prayer involves a time of fellowshipping with the Father.

In Ephesians 6, we are instructed to take the sword of the Spirit, which is the Word of God, and "pray at all times (on every occasion, in every season) in the Spirit, with all [manner of] prayer and entreaty" (Eph. 6:18 AMP).

In 1 Timothy 2 we are admonished and urged that "petitions, prayers, intercessions, and thanksgivings be offered on behalf of all men" (1 Tim. 2:1 AMP). *Prayer is our responsibility.*

Prayer must be the foundation of every Christian endeavor. Any failure is a prayer failure. We are not to be ignorant concerning God's Word. God desires for His people to be successful, to be filled with a full, deep, and clear knowledge of His will (His Word), and to bear fruit in every good work (Col. 1:9,10 AMP). We can then bring honor and glory to Him (John 15:8). He desires that we know how to pray, for "the prayer of the upright is his delight" (Prov. 15:8).

Our Father has not left us helpless. Not only has He given us His Word, He has also given us the Holy Spirit to help our infirmities when we know not how to pray as we ought (Rom. 8:26). Praise God! Our Father has provided His people with every possible avenue to ensure their complete and total victory in this life in the name of our Lord Jesus (1 John 5:3-5).

We pray to the Father, in the name of Jesus, through the Holy Spirit, according to the Word!

Using God's Word on purpose, specifically, in prayer is one means of prayer, and it is a most effective and accurate means. Jesus said, "The words (truths) that I have been speaking to you are spirit and life" (John 6:63 AMP).

When Jesus faced Satan in the wilderness, He said, "It is written...it is written...it is written..." (Matt. 4:4,7,10). We are to live, be upheld, and be sustained by every word that proceeds from the mouth of God (v. 4).

James, by the Spirit, admonishes that we do not have, because we do not ask. We ask and receive not, because we "ask amiss" (James 4:2,3). We must heed that admonishment now, for we are to become experts in prayer, "rightly dividing the word of truth" (2 Tim. 2:15).

Using the Word of God in prayer is *not* taking it out of context, for His Word in us is the key to answered prayer—to prayer that brings results. He "is able to do exceedingly abundantly above all that we ask or think, according to the power that works in us" (Eph. 3:20 NKJV). The power lies within God's Word. The Spirit of God does not lead us apart from the Word, for the Word is of the Spirit of God. We apply that Word personally to ourselves and to others—not adding to or taking from it—in the name of Jesus. We apply the Word to the *now*—to those things, circumstances, and situations facing each of us *now*.

Paul was very specific and definite in his praying. The first chapters of Ephesians, Philippians, Colossians, and

2 Thessalonians are examples of how Paul prayed for believers. There are numerous others. *Search them out.* Paul wrote under the inspiration of the Holy Spirit. We can use these Spirit-given prayers today!

In 2 Corinthians 1:11, 2 Corinthians 9:14, and Philippians 1:4, we see examples of how believers prayed one for another—putting others first in their prayer life with *joy.* Our faith does work by love (Gal. 5:6). We grow spiritually as we reach out to help others—praying for and with them and holding out to them the Word of Life (Phil. 2:16 AMP).

Man is a spirit, he has a soul, and he lives in a body (1 Thess. 5:23). In order to operate successfully, each of these three parts must be fed properly. The soul, or intellect, feeds on intellectual food to produce intellectual strength. The body feeds on physical food to produce physical strength. The spirit—the heart or inward man—is the real person, the part that has been reborn in Christ Jesus. It must feed on spiritual food, which is God's Word, in order to produce and develop faith. As we feast upon God's Word, our minds become renewed with His Word, and we have "a fresh mental and spiritual attitude" (Eph. 4:23,24 AMP).

Likewise, we are to present our bodies "a living sacrifice, holy, acceptable unto God" (Rom. 12:1). We are not to let the body dominate us, but we are to bring it into subjection to our spirit man (1 Cor. 9:27; Eph. 3:16; 1 Pet. 3:4). God's

Word is healing and health to all our flesh (Prov. 4:22 AMP). Therefore, God's Word affects each part of us—spirit, soul, and body. We become vitally united to the Father, to Jesus, and to the Holy Spirit—one with each Person of the Holy Trinity (John 16:13-15; John 17:20-22; Col. 2:6-10).

Purpose to hear, accept, and welcome the Word, and it will take root within your spirit and save your soul. Believe the Word, speak the Word, and act on the Word—it is a creative force. The Word is sharper than a double-edged sword (Heb. 4:12). Often it places a demand on you to change attitudes and behaviors toward the person for whom you are praying.

"Be doers of the word, and not hearers only, deceiving yourselves" (James 1:22 NKJV). Faith without works, or corresponding actions, is *dead* (James 2:17 AMP). Don't be like the mental assenters—those who agree that the Bible is true but who never act on it. *Real faith is acting on God's Word now.* We cannot build faith without practicing the Word. We cannot develop an effective prayer life that is anything but empty words unless God's Word actually has a part in our lives. We are to hold fast to our *confession* of the Word's truthfulness. (Heb. 10:23.) Our Lord Jesus is "the High Priest of our confession" (Heb. 3:1 NKJV), and He is "the Guarantee of a better (stronger) agreement [a more excellent and more advantageous covenant]" (Heb. 7:22 AMP).

Prayer does not cause faith to work, but faith causes prayer to work. Therefore, any prayer problem is the result of a lack of knowledge or the presence of doubt—of doubting the integrity of the Word and the ability of God to stand behind His promises or the statements of fact in the Word.

You can spend fruitless hours in prayer if your heart is not prepared beforehand. Preparation of the heart, the spirit, comes from meditation in the Father's Word, meditation on who you are in Christ, what He is to you, and what the Holy Spirit can mean to you as you become God-inside minded. Just as God told Joshua, as you meditate on the Word day and night, and do according to all that is written in it, then you will make your way prosperous and have good success (Josh. 1:8). Attend to God's Word, submit to His sayings, keep them in the center of your heart, and put far away from you any false, dishonest, willful, and contrary talk (Prov. 4:20-24 AMP).

The Holy Spirit is a divine Helper (John 14:26 AMP), and He will direct your prayer and help you pray when you don't know how (Rom. 8:26). When you use God's Word in prayer, this is *not* something you just rush through, uttering once. Do *not* be mistaken. There is nothing "magical" nor "manipulative" about it—no set pattern or device in order to satisfy what you want or think out of your flesh. Instead, you are holding God's

Word before Him. Jesus said to ask the Father in His name (John 15:16).

We expect God's divine intervention while we choose not to look at the things that are seen, but at the things that are unseen, for the things that are seen are subject to change (2 Cor. 4:18).

Prayer based upon the Word rises above the senses, contacts the Author of the Word, and sets His spiritual laws into motion. It is not just saying prayers that gets results, but it is spending time with the Father, learning His wisdom, drawing on His strength, being filled with His quietness, and basking in His love that bring results to our prayers. Praise the Lord!

* * *

The prayers in this book are designed to teach and train you in the art of prayer. As you pray them, you will be reinforcing the prayer armor, which we have been instructed to put on (Eph. 6:11). The fabric from which the armor is made is the Word of God. We are to live by every word that proceeds from the mouth of God (Luke 4:4). We desire the whole counsel of God because we know it changes us. By receiving that counsel, you will be "...transformed (changed) by the [entire] renewal of your mind [by its new ideals and its new attitude], so that you may prove [for yourselves] what is the good and acceptable and perfect will of God, even the thing which is good and acceptable and perfect [in His sight for you]" (Rom. 12:2 AMP).

The Personal Prayers (Part I) may be used as interces-
sory prayer by simply praying them in the third person,
changing the pronouns *I* or *we* to the name of the person
for whom you are interceding and then adjusting the verbs
accordingly. The Holy Spirit is your Helper. Remember
that you cannot control another's will, but your prayers
can prepare the way for the individual to hear and understand truth.

An often-asked question is this: "How many times
should I pray the same prayer?"

The answer is simple: You pray until you know that
the answer is fixed in your heart. After that, you need to
repeat the prayer whenever adverse circumstances or long
delays cause you to be tempted to doubt that your prayer
has been heard and your request granted.

The Word of God is your weapon against the temptation to lose heart and grow weary in your prayer life
(2 Thess. 3:13). When that Word of promise becomes
fixed in your heart, you will find yourself praising, giving
glory to God for the answer, even when the only evidence
you have of that answer is your own faith. Reaffirming
your faith enforces the triumphant victory of our Lord
Jesus Christ.

Another question often asked is this: "When we repeat
prayers more than once, aren't we praying 'vain repetitions'?"

Obviously, such people are referring to the admonition of Jesus when He told His disciples: "And when you pray, do not heap up phrases (multiply words, repeating the same ones over and over) as the Gentiles do, for they think they will be heard for their much speaking" (Matt. 6:7 AMP). Praying the Word of God is not praying the kind of prayer that the "heathen" pray. You will note in 1 Kings 18:25-29 the manner of prayer that was offered to the gods who could not hear. That is not the way you and I pray. The words that we speak are not vain, but they are spirit and life (John 6:63) and mighty through God to the pulling down of strongholds. (2 Cor. 10:4.) We have a God Whose eyes are over the righteous and Whose ears are open to us (Ps. 34:15): When we pray, He hears us (1 John 5:14,15).

You are the righteousness of God in Christ Jesus (1 Cor. 1:30), and your prayers will avail much (James 5:16). They will bring salvation to the sinner, deliverance to the oppressed, healing to the sick, and prosperity to the poor. They will usher in the next move of God on the earth. In addition to affecting outward circumstances and other people, your prayers will also affect you.

In the very process of praying, your life will be changed as you go from faith to faith (Rom. 1:17) and from glory to glory (2 Cor. 3:18).

As a Christian, your first priority is to love the Lord your God with your entire being and your neighbor as

yourself (Mark 12:30,31). You are called to be an intercessor, a man or woman of prayer (1 Tim. 2:1). You are to
seek the face of the Lord as you inquire, listen, meditate,
and consider in the temple of the Lord (Ps. 27:4 AMP).

As one of "God's set-apart ones" (Acts 20:32 AMP),
the will of the Lord for your life is the same as it is for the
life of every other true believer: "Seek ye first the kingdom
of God, and his righteousness; and all these things shall
be added unto you" (Matt. 6:33).

Personal Confessions

Jesus is Lord over my spirit, my soul, and my body (Phil. 2:9-11).

Jesus has been made unto me wisdom, righteousness, sanctification, and redemption. I can do all things through Christ Who strengthens me (1 Cor. 1:30; Phil. 4:13 NKJV).

The Lord is my Shepherd. I do not want. My God supplies all my need according to His riches in glory in Christ Jesus (Ps. 23:1; Phil. 4:19).

I do not fret or have anxiety about anything. I do not have a care (Phil. 4:6 AMP; 1 Pet. 5:6,7).

I am the Body of Christ. I am redeemed from the curse, because Jesus bore my sicknesses and carried my diseases in His own body. By His stripes I am healed. I forbid any sickness or disease to operate in my body. Every organ, every tissue of my body, functions in the perfection in which God created it to function. I honor God and bring glory to Him in my body (Gal. 3:13; Matt. 8:17 NIV; 1 Pet. 2:24; 1 Cor. 6:20 AMP).

I have the mind of Christ and hold the thoughts, feelings, and purposes of His heart (1 Cor. 2:16 AMP).

I am a believer and not a doubter. I hold fast to my confession of faith. I decide to walk by faith and practice faith. My faith comes by hearing, and hearing by the

Word of God. Jesus is the Author and Finisher (or Developer) of my faith (Heb. 4:14 NKJV; Heb. 11:6; Rom. 10:17 NKJV; Heb. 12:2).

The Holy Spirit has shed the love of God abroad in my heart, and His love abides in me richly. I keep myself in the Kingdom of light, in love, in the Word; and the wicked one touches me not (Rom. 5:5; 1 John 4:16; 1 Tim. 6:17; 1 John 5:18).

I tread upon serpents and scorpions and have power over all the power of the enemy. I take my shield of faith and quench his every fiery dart. Greater is He Who is in me than he who is in the world (Luke 10:19; Eph. 6:16; 1 John 4:4 NKJV).

I am delivered from this present evil world. I am seated with Christ in heavenly places. I reside in the Kingdom of God's dear Son. The law of the Spirit of life in Christ Jesus has made me free from the law of sin and death (Gal. 1:4; Eph. 2:6; Col. 1:13; Rom. 8:2).

I fear *not*, for God has given me a spirit of power, and of love, and of a sound mind. God is on my side (2 Tim. 1:7; Rom. 8:31 AMP).

I hear the voice of the Good Shepherd. I hear my Father's voice, and the voice of a stranger I will not follow. I roll my works upon the Lord. I commit and trust them wholly to Him. He will cause my thoughts to become agreeable to His will, and so shall my plans be established and succeed (John 10:1-5,11,14,27; Prov. 16:3 AMP).

I am a world-overcomer because I am born of God. I represent the Father and Jesus well. I am a useful member in the Body of Christ. I am His workmanship recreated in Christ Jesus. My God is all the while effectually at work in me both to will and to work for His good pleasure (1 John 5:4,5; 2 Cor. 5:20 AMP; Eph. 2:10 AMP; Phil. 2:13 AMP).

I let the Word dwell in me richly. He Who began a good work in me will continue until the day of Christ (Col. 3:16; Phil. 1:6 AMP).

Part I

PERSONAL PRAYERS

Abiding in Jesus

Introduction

Let no one say when he is tempted, I am tempted from God; for God is incapable of being tempted by [what is] evil and He Himself tempts no one.

But every person is tempted when he is drawn away, enticed and baited by his own evil desire (lust, passions).

Then the evil desire, when it has conceived, gives birth to sin, and sin, when it is fully matured, brings forth death.

James 1:13-15 AMP

Single people sometimes express the difficulty of keeping themselves pure. (See the following prayers on purity.) Some have asked, "Doesn't God understand that we are only human? Why did He create us with desires? Surely He understands and excuses us when we fall into temptation. If He wants me to avoid sexual temptation, then why doesn't He send me the spouse I have asked Him to give me?"

The Scriptures condemn premarital sex, fornication, adultery, and all forms of sexual perversion (Matt. 15:19; Mark 7:21 AMP; Gal. 5:19-21; Col. 3:5,6). Although sexual desires are not a sin, if not properly controlled, those desires can lead to sin.

According to James 1:13-15, sin begins with a thought conceived from lust. Lust is not limited to sex. It is possible to lust after many things that can cause sin. That's why it is so important to take control over the mind and heart to keep them pure and holy—in spite of temptation.

One of the myths that has ensnared many single people is the mistaken idea that marriage will automatically release them from the temptation to sin. Without repentance and the renewing of the mind, those who have a problem with lustful thoughts before they are married will have the same problem after they are married, just as those who have a problem with sexual perversion before marriage will continue to have the same problem after marriage.

One married man shared his testimony of deliverance from pornography. Yet He still had to continually guard himself from mental images that kept reappearing.

Marriage is not a cure-all for sexual sins or any other sin.

Yes, God does understand. With every temptation He has provided a way of escape (1 Cor. 10:13).

Yes, there is forgiveness for sin (1 John 1:9)—through God's abounding grace (Rom. 5:20). The question is, "...Are we to remain in sin in order that God's grace (favor and mercy) may multiply and overflow? Certainly not! How can we who died to sin live in it any longer?" (Rom. 6:1,2 AMP).

We who are in Christ desire to bring glory to the Father. We cannot do so in our own strength. It is abiding in union with Jesus and loving as Jesus loves that ensures answered prayers. (John 15:7-9 AMP). If our prayers are not being answered, it is time to check our love walk. We must ask ourselves, "Are we keeping ourselves in the love of God—remaining vitally united with Jesus?"

> We know [absolutely] that anyone born of God does not [deliberately and knowingly] practice committing sin, but the One Who was begotten of God carefully watches over and protects him [Christ's divine presence within him preserves him against the evil], and the wicked one does not lay hold (get a grip) on him or touch [him].

> 1 John 5:18 AMP

This verse says that the wicked one cannot touch us. What is the condition? Having Christ's presence within, staying united with Him—abiding in Him and allowing His Word to abide in us.

If you want to abide in Christ and have His Word abide in you, pray the following prayer with a sincere and believing heart.

Prayer

Lord, I am abiding in Your Word [holding fast to Your teachings and living in accordance with them]. It is my desire to be Your true disciple. I am abiding in (vitally united to) the vine. I cannot bear fruit unless I abide in You.

Lord, because You are the Vine, and I am a branch living in You, I bear much (abundant) fruit. Apart from You [cut off from vital union with You] I can do nothing. Your Son, Jesus, said, "If you live in Me [abide vitally united to Me] and My words remain in you and continue to live in your hearts, ask whatever you will, and it shall be done for you" (John 15:7 AMP).

When I bear (produce) much fruit, You, Father, are honored and glorified. By Your grace that I have received, I will show and prove myself to be a true follower of Your Son, Jesus. He has loved me, [just] as You, Father, have loved Him. I am abiding in that love.

Lord, You have assured me that if I keep Your commandments [if I continue to obey Your instructions], I will abide in Your love and live in it, just as Your Son, Jesus, obeyed Your commandments and lived in Your love. He told me these things, that Your joy and delight may be in me and that my joy and gladness may be of full measure and complete and overflowing. This is Your commandment: that we love one another [just] as You have loved us.

Father, thank You for Your Word—it is the truth that makes me free. I am born (begotten) of You, Lord, and I do not [deliberately, knowingly, and habitually] practice sin. Your nature abides in me [Your principle of life remains permanently within me]; and I cannot practice sinning because I am born (begotten) of You. I have hidden Your Word in my heart that I might not sin against You.

May Christ through my faith [actually] dwell (settle down, abide, make His permanent home) in my heart! It is my desire to be rooted deep in love and founded securely on love, that I may have the power and be strong to apprehend and grasp with all the saints [Your devoted people, the experience of that love] what is the breadth and length and height and depth [of it].

I pray, in the name of Jesus, that I may know this love that surpasses knowledge—that I may be filled to the measure of all Your fullness. You are able to do immeasurably more than all I ask or imagine, according to Your power that is at work within me. To You be glory in the Church and in Christ Jesus throughout all generations, forever and ever! Amen.

Scripture References

John 8:31 AMP	1 John 3:9 AMP
John 15:4,5 AMP	Psalm 119:11
John 15:7-12 AMP	Ephesians 3:17,18 AMP
John 8:32	Ephesians 3:19-21 NIV
John 17:17	

To Walk in the Word

Father, in the name of Jesus, *I commit myself to walk in the Word.* Your Word living in me produces Your life in this world. I recognize that Your Word is integrity itself—steadfast, sure, eternal—and I trust my life to its provisions.

You have sent Your Word forth into my heart. I let it dwell in me richly in all wisdom. I meditate in it day and night so that I may diligently act on it. The Incorruptible Seed, the Living Word, the Word of Truth, is abiding in my spirit. That Seed is growing mightily in me now, producing Your nature, Your life. It is my counsel, my shield, my buckler, my powerful weapon in battle. The Word is a lamp to my feet and a light to my path. It makes my way plain before me. I do not stumble, for my steps are ordered in the Word.

The Holy Spirit leads and guides me into all the truth. He gives me understanding, discernment, and comprehension so that I am preserved from the snares of the evil one.

I delight myself in You and Your Word. Because of that, You put Your desires within my heart. I commit my way unto You, and You bring it to pass. I am confident that You are at work in me now both to will and to do all Your good pleasure.

I exalt Your Word, hold it in high esteem, and give it first place. *I make my schedule around Your Word.* I make the Word the final authority to settle all questions that confront me. I choose to agree with the Word of God, and I choose to disagree with any thoughts, conditions, or circumstances contrary to Your Word. I boldly and confidently say that my heart is fixed and established on the solid foundation—the Living Word of God! Amen.

Scripture References

Colossians 3:16	Psalm 37:4,5
Joshua 1:8	Philippians 2:13 AMP
1 Peter 1:23	Colossians 3:15 AMP
Psalm 119:105	2 Corinthians 10:5
Psalm 37:23	Psalm 112:7,8
John 16:13	

For Confidence in Your Prayers

Heavenly Father, You are my God and early will I seek You, knowing that You hear the cry of the righteous. You are my hope, Sovereign Lord. You are my confidence, and You will keep my foot from being snared. I have been made the righteousness of God in Christ Jesus, and my prayers avail much.

Jesus is the Way into the Holy of Holies and the High Priest of my confession. I have confidence to enter the Most Holy Place by the blood of Jesus. In Christ Jesus and through faith in Him I approach You, my Father, with freedom and confidence. If I ask anything according to Your will, You hear me. And if I know that You hear me, whatever I ask, I know that I have what I have asked of You.

On the authority of Your Word, I believe that when I do not know what I ought to pray for, the Holy Spirit Himself intercedes for me with groans that words cannot express. He searches my heart knowing the mind of the Spirit, and intercedes for me in accordance with Your will. And I know that in all things You are working for my good because I love You. You called me according to Your purpose, chose me before the foundation of the world to be holy and without blame before You in love.

In the name of Jesus I will not throw away my confidence; it will be richly rewarded. I will persevere so that when I have done Your will, I will receive what You have promised. I am Your righteous one who is living by faith in the name of Jesus. Amen.

Scripture References

Psalm 63:1 NKJV	Hebrews 3:1 NAS
Psalm 34:17	Hebrews 10:19-25 NLT
Psalm 55:17,18	1 John 5:14,15 NKJV
Psalm 71:5	Romans 8:26-28 NIV
Proverbs 3:26 NIV	Ephesians 1:4
1 Corinthians 1:30	Hebrews 10:35,36 NIV
James 5:16	Galatians 2:20

To Be God-Inside Minded

I am a spirit learning to live in a natural world. I have a soul, and I live in a physical body. I am in the world, but I am not of the world. God of peace, I ask You to sanctify me in every way, and may my whole spirit and soul and body be kept blameless until that day when our Lord Jesus Christ comes again. Father, You called me, and You are completely dependable. You said it, and You will do it. Thank You for the Spirit Who guides me into all truth through my regenerated human spirit.

Lord, Your searchlight penetrates my human spirit, exposing every hidden motive. You actually gave me Your Spirit (not the world's spirit) so I can know the wonderful things You have given to me. I am Your child, born of Your Spirit, filled with Your Spirit, and led by Your Spirit. I listen to my heart as I look to the Spirit inside me.

Thank You, Holy Spirit, for directing me and illuminating my mind. You lead me in the way I should go in all the affairs of life. You lead me by an inward witness. The eyes of my understanding are being enlightened. Wisdom is in my inward parts. God's love is perfected in me. I have an unction from the Holy One.

Father, I am becoming spirit-conscious. I listen to the voice of my spirit and obey what my spirit tells me. My spirit is controlled by the Holy Spirit and dominates me, for I walk not after the flesh, but after the Spirit. I examine my leading in the light of the Word.

I trust in You, Lord, with all of my heart and lean not to my own understanding. In all of my ways I acknowledge You, and You direct my paths. I walk in the light of the Word. Holy Spirit, You are my Counselor, teaching me to educate, train, and develop my human spirit. The Word of God shall not depart out of my mouth. I meditate therein day and night. Therefore, I will make my way prosperous, and I will have good success in life. I am a doer of the Word, and I put Your Word first.

In Jesus' name, amen.

Scripture References

1 Thessalonians 5:23,24	1 John 4:12
John 16:13	1 John 2:20
1 Peter 1:23 AMP	Romans 8:1
Proverbs 20:27 NLT	Proverbs 3:5,6
1 Corinthians 2:12 NLT	Psalm 119:105
Romans 8:14,16	John 14:26
John 3:6,7	Joshua 1:8
Ephesians 5:18	James 1:22
Isaiah 48:17	Ephesians 1:18

To Obtain and Maintain Godly Character

Father, I desire to receive wisdom and discipline. I ask for the ability to understand words of insight. By Your grace, I am acquiring a disciplined and prudent life, doing what is right and just and fair.

Thank You for giving me prudence, knowledge, and discretion. As a wise person I listen and add to my learning, and as a discerning person I accept guidance [so that I may be able to steer my course rightly].

Thank You that I understand proverbs and parables, the sayings and riddles of the wise.

In Jesus' name I pray, amen.

Scripture References

Proverbs 1:2-7 NIV   Proverbs 1:5 AMP

To Walk in God's Wisdom and His Perfect Will

Lord and God, You are worthy to receive glory and honor and power, for You created all things, and by Your will they were created and have their being. You adopted me as Your child through Jesus Christ, in accordance with Your pleasure and will. I pray that I may be active in sharing my faith, so that I will have a full understanding of every good thing I have in Christ.

Father, I ask You to give me a complete understanding of what You want to do in my life, and I ask You to make me wise with spiritual wisdom. Then the way I live will always honor and please You, and I will continually do good, kind things for others. All the while, I will learn to know You better and better.

I roll my works upon You, Lord, and You cause my thoughts to become agreeable to Your will, so that my plans are established and succeed. You direct my steps and make them sure. I understand and firmly grasp what Your will is for me. In the name of Jesus, I am not vague, thoughtless, or foolish. I stand firm and mature [in spiritual growth], convinced and fully assured in everything willed by You.

Father, You have destined and appointed me to come progressively to know Your will [to perceive, to recognize more strongly and clearly, and to become better and more intimately acquainted with Your will]. I thank You, Father, for the Holy Spirit Who abides permanently in me and Who guides me into all the Truth (the whole, full Truth) and Who speaks whatever He hears [from You, Father] and announces and declares to me the things that are to come. I have the mind of Christ and do hold the thoughts, feelings, and purposes of His heart.

So, Father, I have entered into Your blessed rest by adhering to, trusting in, and relying on You, in the name of Jesus. Hallelujah! Amen.

Scripture References

Revelation 4:11 NIV

Ephesians 5:17 AMP

Ephesians 1:5 NIV

Colossians 4:12 AMP

Philemon 6

Acts 22:14 AMP

Colossians 1:9,10 NLT

1 Corinthians 2:16 AMP

Proverbs 16:3,9 AMP

Hebrews 4:10

To Trust in the Lord

Devotional Reading

For all God's words are right, and everything
he does is worthy of our trust. He loves whatever
is just and good; the earth is filled with his tender
love. He merely spoke, and the heavens were
formed, and all the galaxies of stars. He made the
oceans, pouring them into his vast reservoirs.

Let everyone in all the world—men, women
and children—fear the Lord and stand in awe of
him. For when he but spoke, the world began! It
appeared at his command! And with a breath he
can scatter the plans of all the nations who oppose
him, but his own plan stands forever. His inten-
tions are the same for every generation.

Psalm 33:4-11 TLB

Prayer

Father, I ask for grace to trust You more. When I am
afraid I will trust in You. I praise Your Word. My God, in
You I trust; I will not be afraid. What can mortal man do
to me?

Lord, Your steadfast love never ceases; Your mercies
never come to an end; they are new every morning; great

is Your faithfulness. You are my portion; therefore, I will hope in You.

May You, the God of hope, fill me with all joy and peace as I trust in You, so that I may overflow with hope by the power of the Holy Spirit.

To You, O Lord, I pray and according to Your Word You will not fail me, for I am trusting You. None who has faith in You, Father, will ever be disgraced for trusting You.

Show me the path where I should go, O Lord; point out the right road for me to walk. Lead me; teach me; for You are the God Who gives me salvation.

Lord, I have no fear of bad news; my heart is steadfast, trusting in You. My heart is secure; I will have no fear.

Because You are faithful and trustworthy, I make a commitment to trust in You with all my heart and lean not on my own understanding; in all my ways I acknowledge You, and You will make my paths straight. I am blessed, for I trust in the Lord, in Whom is my confidence.

In Jesus' name I pray, amen.

Scripture References

Psalm 56:3,4 NIV   Psalm 112:7,8 NIV

Lamentations 3:22-24 RSV   Proverbs 3:5,6 NIV

Romans 15:13 NIV   Jeremiah 17:7 NIV

Psalm 25:1-5 TLB

To Give Thanks to God

Introduction

God saw you when you were in your mother's womb
(Ps. 139:13-16). He knew your mother and father and the
circumstances of the home where you were to grow up.
He knew the schools you would attend and the neighbor-
hood in which you would live.

God gave you the ability to survive and walked with
you through good times and bad. He gave you survival
techniques and guardian angels to keep and protect you
(Ps. 91:11). He chose you before the foundation of the
world to be holy and without blame before Him in love
(Eph. 1:4).

He cried with you when you cried. He laughed with you
when you laughed. He was grieved when you were misun-
derstood and treated unfairly. He watched and waited,
looking forward to the day when you would receive Jesus
as your Savior. To as many as received Him He gave the
power, the right, and the authority to become the children
of God (John 1:12 AMP). He longs for your fellowship,
desiring for you to know Him more and more intimately.

Your survival techniques were probably different from
mine. Whatever they were, and whatever your life may
have been like up to this point, the peace of God can

change the regrets and the wounds of the past into thanksgiving and praise. You can experience wholeness by earnestly and sincerely praying this prayer.

I.

Daily Prayer of Thanksgiving

Father, I come to You in the name of Jesus. With the help of the Holy Spirit and by Your grace, I join with the heavenly host making a joyful noise to You and serving You with gladness! I come before Your presence with singing!

Lord, I know (perceive, recognize, and understand with approval) that You are God! It is You who made us, not we ourselves [and we are Yours]! We are Your people and the sheep of Your pasture.

Father, I enter into Your gates with thanksgiving and present an offering of thanks. I enter into Your courts with praise! I am thankful and delight to say so. I bless and affectionately praise Your name! For You are good, and Your mercy and loving-kindness are everlasting. Your faithfulness and truth endure to all generations. It is a good and delightful thing to give thanks to You, O Most High.

Lord, by Your Holy Spirit, perfect the fruit of my lips. Help me draw thanksgiving forth from my innermost resources; reach down into the most secret places of my heart that I may offer significant thanksgiving to You, Father.

Thank You for my parents who gave me life. I am grateful for the victories and achievements I have experienced in spite of my hurts—the bruises and the abuses that boxed me in when I was a small child. You used them for good even though Satan intended them for my destruction.

You prepared me to listen to the inner voice—the voice of Your Holy Spirit.

Thank You for Your grace, which is teaching me to trust myself and others. Thank You for life—life in all its abundance.

It was You Who gave me a desire to pray, and I am grateful for the prayer closet where we meet. I thank You for Your Word. Life is exciting, and I am grateful that I am alive for such a time as this.

Thank You for past and present relationships. I learn from those who oppose me and from those who are for me. You are teaching me to recognize and understand my strengths and weaknesses. Thank You for giving me discernment and spiritual understanding. I enter Your gates with thanksgiving in my heart.

You are my Father. I am Your child, loved by You unconditionally. I rejoice in You, Lord, and give thanks at the remembrance of Your holiness.

I am an overcomer by the blood of the Lamb and by the word of my testimony.

In the name of Jesus, amen.

Scripture References

Psalm 100:1-5 AMP	Philippians 2:13
Psalm 92:1 AMP	Esther 4:14
Psalm 138:8	Psalm 100:4
Hebrews 13:15	Philippians 3:1
Genesis 50:20 NIV	Psalm 30:4
John 10:10	Revelation 12:11

II.

Prayer of Thanksgiving for Food Eaten While Traveling

Father, I ask for the wisdom to order that which is healthy and nourishing to my body.

In the name of Jesus, I resist the lust of the flesh and the lust of the eye as I scan the menu. When I am in doubt about what I am to order, I will pause and ask for wisdom, which You will give generously without finding fault with me.

Should I unknowingly eat or drink any deadly thing, it will not harm me, for the Spirit of life makes me free from the law of sin and death.

Everything You have created, Father, is good, and nothing is to be thrown away or refused if it is received with thanksgiving. It is hallowed and consecrated by Your Word and by prayer.

I receive this food with thanksgiving and will eat the amount that is sufficient for me.

In the name of Jesus, amen.

Scripture References

1 John 2:16	Romans 8:2
James 1:5	1 Timothy 4:4,5 AMP
Mark 16:18	Psalm 136:1,25

Complete in God as a Single

Father, I thank You that I desire and earnestly seek first after the things of Your Kingdom. I thank You that I know that You love me and that I can trust Your Word.

For in Jesus the whole fullness of diety (the Godhead) continues to dwell in bodily form [giving complete expression of Your divine nature], and I am in Him and have come to the fullness of life [in Christ. In Him I am filled with the Godhead—Father, Son, and Holy Spirit—and I reach full spiritual stature]. And He is the Head of all rule and authority [of every angelic principality and power].

So because of Jesus, I am complete; Jesus is my Lord. I come before You, Father, desiring a born-again, Christian mate; nevertheless, I petition that Your will be done in my life. Now I enter into Your blessed rest by adhering to, trusting in, and relying on You, in the name of Jesus, amen.

Scripture References

Matthew 6:33 AMP   Hebrews 4:10 AMP

Colossians 2:9,10 AMP

Part II

PRAYERS FOR
VICTORY EVERY DAY

To Submit to God

Father, You are the Supreme Authority—a God of order. You have instituted other authority structures that will support healthy relationships and maintain harmony. It is my decision to surrender my will to You, that I might find protection and dwell in the secret place of the Most High.

Father, thank You for pastors and leaders of the church—those who are submitted to You and are examples to the congregation. I submit to the church elders (the ministers and spiritual guides of the church)—[giving them due respect and yielding to their counsel].

Lord, You know just how rebellious I have been. I ask Your forgiveness for manipulating circumstances and people—for trying to manipulate You to get my own way. May Your will be done in my life, even as it is in heaven.

Father, when I feel that my life is spiraling out of control, I bind my mind to the mind of Christ, and my emotions to the control of the Holy Spirit. I loose my mind from obsessive thought patterns that try to confuse me.

Obedience is far better than sacrifice. Father, You are much more interested in my listening to You than in my offerings of material things to You. Rebellion is as bad as the sin of witchcraft, and stubbornness is as bad as worshiping idols. Forgive me for practicing witchcraft and worshiping idols.

Father, You deserve honesty from the heart; yes, utter sincerity and truthfulness. Oh, give me this wisdom. Sprinkle me with the cleansing blood, and I shall be clean again. Wash me, and I shall be whiter than snow. You have rescued me from the dominion of darkness and brought me into the Kingdom of the Son You love, in Whom I have redemption, the forgiveness of sins.

Lord, I want to follow You. I am putting aside my own desires and conveniences. I yield my desires that are not in Your plan for me. Even in the midst of my fear, I surrender and entrust my future to You. I choose to take up my cross and follow You [cleave steadfastly to You, conforming wholly to Your example in living and, if need be, in dying also]. I desire to lose my [lower] life on Your account that I might find it [the higher life].

Father, You gave Jesus to be my Example. He has returned to You, Father, and has sent the Holy Spirit to be my Helper and Guide. In this world there are temptations, trials, and tribulations; but Jesus has overcome the world, and I am of good cheer.

Jesus is my Lord. I choose to become His servant. He calls me His friend.

Lord, help me to walk through the process of surrendering my all to You. I exchange rebellion and stubbornness for a willing and obedient heart. When I refuse to listen, anoint my ears to hear; when I am blinded by my own desires, open my eyes to see.

I belong to Jesus Christ, the Anointed One, Who breaks down and destroys every yoke of bondage. In His name and in obedience to Your will, Father, I submit to the control and direction of the Holy Spirit Whom You have sent to live in me. I am Your child. All to You I surrender. I am an overcomer by the blood of the Lamb and by the word of my testimony!

In Jesus' name I pray, amen.

Scripture References

1 Corinthians 14:33	Psalm 51:6,7 TLB
1 Timothy 2:2	Colossians 1:13,14 NIV
Psalm 91:1	Matthew 10:38,39 AMP
1 Peter 5:5 AMP	John 14:26 AMP
Matthew 6:10	John 16:13 AMP
Matthew 18:18	John 16:33
1 Corinthians 2:16	John 15:15
James 4:7	Revelation 12:11
1 Samuel 15:22,23 TLB	

To Please God Rather Than Man

Father, I desire to please You rather than men. Forgive me for loving the approval and the praise and the glory that come from men [instead of and] more than the glory that comes from You. [I value my credit with You more than my credit with men.]

In Jesus' name I declare that I am free from the fear of man, which brings a snare. I lean on, trust in, and put my confidence in You. I am safe and set on high.

I take comfort and am encouraged and confidently and boldly say, "The Lord is my Helper; I will not be seized with alarm [I will not fear or dread or be terrified]. What can man do to me?" (Heb. 13:6 AMP).

Father, just as You sent Jesus into the world, You have sent me. You are ever with me, for I always seek to do what pleases You.

In Jesus' name, amen.

Scripture References

John 12:43 AMP	John 17:18 AMP
Proverbs 29:25 AMP	John 8:29 AMP
Hebrew 13:6 AMP	

To Renew Your Mind

Father, in Jesus' name, I shall prosper and be in health, even as my soul prospers. I have the mind of Christ (the Messiah) and do hold the thoughts (feelings and purposes) of His heart. I trust in You, Lord, with all my heart; I lean not unto my own understanding, but in all my ways I acknowledge You, and You shall direct my paths.

Today I submit myself to Your Word, which exposes and sifts and analyzes and judges the very thoughts and purposes of my heart. (For the weapons of my warfare are not carnal, but mighty through You to the pulling down of strong-holds—*intimidation, fears, doubts, unbelief, and failure.*) I refute arguments and theories and reasonings and every proud and lofty thing that sets itself up against the (true) knowledge of You; and I lead every thought and purpose away captive into the obedience of Christ (the Messiah, the Anointed One).

Today I shall be transformed by the renewing of my mind, that I may prove what is Your good and acceptable and perfect will. Your Word, Lord, shall not depart out of my mouth; but I shall meditate on it day and night, that I may observe to do according to all that is written therein: for then I shall make my way prosperous, then I shall have good success.

My thoughts are the thoughts of the diligent, which tend only to plenteousness. Therefore, I am not anxious

about anything, but in everything by prayer and petition,*
with thanksgiving, I present my requests to You. And Your
peace, which transcends all understanding, will guard my
heart and my mind in Christ Jesus.

Today I fix my mind on whatever is *true,* whatever is
worthy of reverence and is *honorable* and *seemly,* whatever is
just, whatever is *pure,* whatever is *lovely* and *lovable,* whatever is *kind* and *winsome* and *gracious.* If there is any *virtue*
and *excellence,* if there is anything *worthy of praise,* I will
think on and weigh and take account of these things [fix
my mind on them].

Today I roll my works upon You, Lord [I commit and
trust them wholly to You; You will cause my thoughts to
become agreeable to Your will, and] so shall my plans be
established and succeed.

In Jesus' name I pray, amen.

Scripture References

3 John 2	Romans 12:2
1 Corinthians 2:16 AMP	Joshua 1:8
Proverbs 3:5,6	Proverbs 21:5
Hebrews 4:12 AMP	Philippians 4:6,7 NIV
2 Corinthians 10:4	Philippians 4:8 AMP
2 Corinthians 10:5 AMP	Proverbs 16:3 AMP

* I encourage you to keep a prayer journal, writing down your petitions
(definite requests) in prayer form.

To Put on the Armor of God

In the name of Jesus, I put on the whole armor of God, that I may be able to stand against the wiles of the devil. For I wrestle not against flesh and blood, but against principalities, powers, the rulers of the darkness of this world, and spiritual wickedness in high places.

Therefore, I take unto myself the whole armor of God that I may be able to withstand in the evil day, and having done all, to stand. I stand, therefore, having my loins girt about with truth. Your Word, Lord, which is truth, contains all the weapons of my warfare, which are not carnal, but mighty through You to the pulling down of strongholds.

I have on the breastplate of integrity and of moral rectitude and right standing with You, which is faith and love. My feet are shod with the preparation of the Gospel of peace. In Christ Jesus I have peace and pursue peace with all men. I am a minister of reconciliation, proclaiming the good news of the Gospel.

I take the shield of faith, upon which I can quench all the flaming missiles of the wicked [one]; the helmet of salvation *(holding the thoughts, feelings, and purpose of Your heart, Lord)*; and the sword of the Spirit, which is Your Word. In the face of all trials, tests, temptations, and tribulation, I cut to pieces the snare of the enemy by speaking Your Word. Greater is He Who is in me than he who is in the world.

Thank You, Father, for the armor. I will pray at all times (on every occasion, in every season) in the Spirit, with all [manner of] prayer and entreaty. To that end I will keep alert and watch with strong purpose and perseverance, interceding in behalf of all the saints. My power and ability and sufficiency are from You Who qualified me as a minister and a dispenser of a new covenant [of salvation through Christ]. Amen.

Scripture References

Ephesians 6:11-14	2 Corinthians 5:18
John 17:17	Ephesians 6:16,17 AMP
2 Corinthians 10:4	1 John 4:4
Ephesians 6:14,15 AMP	Ephesians 6:18 AMP
Ephesians 2:14	2 Corinthians 3:5,6 AMP
Psalm 34:14	

To Cast Down Imaginations

Father, though I live in the world, I do not wage war as the world does. The weapons I fight with are not the weapons of the world. On the contrary, they have divine power to demolish strongholds. I demolish arguments and every pretension that sets itself up against the knowledge of You, and I take captive every thought to make it obedient to Christ.

In the name of Jesus, I ask You, Father, to bless those who have despitefully used me. Whenever I feel afraid, I will trust in You. When I feel miserable, I will express thanksgiving; and when I feel that life is unfair, I will remember that You are more than enough.

When I feel ashamed, help me to remember that I no longer have to be afraid; I will not suffer shame. I am delivered from the fear of disgrace; I will not be humiliated. I relinquish the shame of my youth.

It is well with my soul, for You have redeemed me. You have called me by my name, and I overcome evil with good.

I am in Your will for my life at this time. I am being transformed through the renewing of my mind. I am able to test and approve [for myself] what Your will is—Your good and acceptable and perfect will.

You have good things reserved for my future. All my needs will be met according to Your riches in glory. I will replace worry for my family with asking You to protect and care for them.

You are love, and perfect love casts out fear.

In Jesus' name, amen.

Scripture References

2 Corinthians 10:3-5 NIV	Romans 12:21
Luke 6:28	Romans 12:2 AMP
Psalm 56:3	Jeremiah 29:11 AMP
Isaiah 61:3	Philippians 4:19
Psalm 4:6 MESSAGE	1 Peter 5:7
Isaiah 54:4 NIV	John 4:8,18
Isaiah 43:1	

To Conquer the Thought Life

In the name of Jesus, I take authority over my thought life. Even though I walk (live) in the flesh, I am not carrying on my warfare according to the flesh and using mere human weapons. For the weapons of my warfare are not physical [weapons of flesh and blood], but they are mighty before God, for the overthrow and destruction of strongholds. I refute arguments and theories and reasonings and every proud and lofty thing that sets itself up against the (true) knowledge of God; and I lead every thought and purpose away captive into the obedience of Christ (the Messiah, the Anointed One).

With my soul I will bless You, Lord, with every thought and purpose in life. My mind will not wander out of Your presence. My life will glorify You, Father—*spirit, soul, and body.* I take no account of the evil done to me [I pay no attention to a suffered wrong]. It holds no place in my thought life. I am ever ready to believe the best of every person. I gird up the loins of my mind, and I set my mind and keep it set on what is above (the higher things), not on the things that are on the earth.

Whatever is true, whatever is worthy of reverence and is honorable and seemly, whatever is just, whatever is pure, whatever is lovely and lovable, whatever is kind and winsome and gracious, if there is any virtue and excellence, if there is anything worthy of praise, I will think on and weigh and take account of these things [I will fix my mind on them].

I have the mind of Christ (the Messiah), and do hold the thoughts (feelings and purposes) of His heart. In the name of Jesus, I will practice what I have learned and received and heard and seen in Christ, and will model my way of living on it, and the God of peace (of untroubled, undisturbed well-being) will be with me.

In Jesus' name, amen.

Scripture References

2 Corinthians 10:3-5 AMP

Psalm 103:1 AMP

1 Corinthians 6:20 AMP

1 Corinthians 13:5,7 AMP

1 Peter 1:13 AMP

Colossians 3:2 AMP

Philippians 4:8 AMP

1 Corinthians 2:16 AMP

Philippians 4:9 AMP

To Watch What You Say

Father, today I make a commitment to You in the
name of Jesus. I turn from speaking idle words and fool-
ishly speaking things that are contrary to my true desire to
myself and toward others. Your Word says that the tongue
defiles, that the tongue sets on fire the course of nature,
that the tongue is set on fire of hell.

*In the name of Jesus, I submit to godly wisdom that I
might learn to control my tongue.* I am determined that hell
will not set my tongue on fire. I renounce, reject, and
repent of every word that has ever proceeded out of my
mouth against You, Father, and Your operation. I cancel
its power and dedicate my mouth to speak excellent and
right things. My mouth shall utter truth.

Because I am the righteousness of God in Christ
Jesus, I set the course of my life for obedience, for abundance, for wisdom, for health, and for joy. Set a guard over
my mouth, O Lord; keep watch over the door of my lips.
Then the words of my mouth and my deeds shall show
forth Your righteousness and Your salvation all of my
days. I purpose to guard my mouth and my tongue that I
might keep myself from calamity.

Father, Your words are top priority to me. They are
spirit and life. I let Your Word dwell in me richly in all
wisdom. Your ability is released within me by the words of

my mouth and by Your Word. I speak Your words out of my mouth. They are alive in me. You are alive and working in me. So, I can boldly say that my words are words of faith, words of power, words of love, and words of life. They produce good things in my life and in the lives of others because I choose Your words for my lips, and Your will for my life, in Jesus' name, amen.

Scripture References

Ephesians 5:4

2 Timothy 2:16

James 3:6

Proverbs 8:6,7

2 Corinthians 5:21

Psalm 141:3 NIV

Proverbs 21:23 NIV

John 6:63

Colossians 3:16

To Walk in Love

Father, in Jesus' name, I thank You that Your love has been poured forth into my heart by the Holy Spirit Who has been given to me. I keep and treasure Your Word. The love of and for You, Father, has been perfected and completed in me; and perfect love casts out all fear.

Father, I am Your child, and *I commit to walk in the God-kind of love.* I endure long; I am patient and kind. I am never envious and never boil over with jealousy. I am not boastful or vainglorious, and I do not display myself haughtily. I am not rude and unmannerly, and I do not act unbecomingly. I do not insist on my own rights or my own way, for I am not self-seeking, touchy, fretful, or resentful. I take no account of an evil done to me, [and I pay no attention to a suffered wrong]. I do not rejoice at injustice and unrighteousness, but I rejoice when right and truth prevail. I bear up under anything and everything that comes. I am ever ready to believe the *best* of others. My hopes are fadeless under all circumstances. I endure everything [without weakening] because Your love in me never fails.

Father, I *bless* and *pray* for those who persecute me [who are cruel in their attitude toward me]. I bless them and do not curse them. Therefore, my love abounds yet more and more in knowledge and in all judgment. I approve things that are excellent. I am sincere and *without offense* till the day of Christ. I am filled with the fruits of righteousness.

Everywhere I go I commit to plant seeds of love. I thank You, Father, for preparing hearts ahead of time to receive this love. I know that these seeds will produce Your love in the hearts to whom they are given.

Father, I thank You that as I flow in Your love and wisdom, people are being blessed by my life and ministry. Father, You make me to find favor, compassion, and loving-kindness with others (*name them*).

I am rooted deep in love and founded securely on love, knowing that You are on my side and that nothing is able to separate me from Your love, Father, which is in Christ Jesus my Lord. Thank You, Father, in Jesus' precious name, amen.

Scripture References

Romans 5:5 AMP

1 John 2:5 AMP

1 John 4:18 AMP

1 Corinthians 13:4-8 AMP

Romans 12:14 AMP

Matthew 5:44 AMP

Philippians 1:9-11 AMP

John 13:34 AMP

1 Corinthians 3:6 AMP

Daniel 1:9 AMP

Ephesians 3:17 AMP

Romans 8:31,39 AMP

To Walk in Forgiveness

Father, in the name of Jesus, I make a fresh commitment to You to live in peace and harmony, not only with the other brothers and sisters of the Body of Christ, but also with my friends, associates, neighbors, and family.

Father, I repent of holding on to bad feelings toward others. I bind myself to godly repentance and loose myself from bitterness, resentment, envying, strife, and unkindness in any form. Father, I ask Your forgiveness for the sin of _____. By faith, I receive it, having assurance that I am cleansed from all unrighteousness through Jesus Christ. I ask You to forgive and release all who have wronged and hurt me. I forgive and release them. Deal with them in Your mercy and loving-kindness.

From this moment on, I purpose to walk in love, to seek peace, to live in agreement, and to conduct myself toward others in a manner that is pleasing to You. I know that I have right standing with You, and Your ears are attentive to my prayers.

It is written in Your Word that Your love has been poured forth into my heart by the Holy Ghost Who is given to me. I believe that love flows forth into the lives of everyone I know, that we may be filled with and abound in the fruits of righteousness, which bring glory and honor unto You, Lord, in Jesus' name. So be it! Amen.

Scripture References

Romans 12:16-18

Romans 12:10

Philippians 2:2

Ephesians 4:31

Ephesians 4:27

John 1:9

Mark 11:25

Ephesians 4:32

1 Peter 3:8,11,12

Colossians 1:10

Romans 5:5

Philippians 1:9,11

To Walk in God's Provision:
"Give Us This Day Our Daily Bread"

In the name of Jesus, I confess with the psalmist David that I have not seen the righteous forsaken, nor his seed begging bread.

Father, thank You for food, clothing, and shelter. In the name of Jesus, I am learning to stop being perpetually uneasy (anxious and worried) about my life, what I shall eat and what I shall drink, or about my body, what I shall put on. My life is greater [in quality] than food, and my body [far above and more excellent] than clothing.

The bread of idleness [gossip, discontent, and self-pity] I will not eat. It is You, Father, Who will liberally supply (fill to the full) my every need according to Your riches in glory in Christ Jesus.

In the name of Jesus, I shall not live by bread alone, but by every word that proceeds from the mouth of God. Your words were found, and I ate them, and Your Word was to me a joy and the rejoicing of my heart.

And the Word became flesh and dwelt among us. Jesus, You are the Bread of Life [that gives me life—the Living Bread].

Thank You, Father, in the name of Jesus, for spiritual bread—manna from heaven. Amen.

Scripture References

Matthew 6:9-11

Psalm 37:25

Matthew 6:25 AMP

Proverbs 31:27 AMP

Philippians 4:19 AMP

Matthew 4:4

Jeremiah 15:16 AMP

John 1:14

John 6:48 AMP

Victory in a Healthy Lifestyle

Father, I am Your child, and Jesus is Lord over my spirit, soul, and body. I praise You because I am fearfully and wonderfully made. Your works are wonderful; I know that full well.

Lord, thank You for declaring Your plans for me—plans to prosper me and not to harm me, plans to give me hope and a future. I choose to renew my mind to Your plans for a healthy lifestyle. You have abounded toward me in all prudence and wisdom. Therefore, I give thought to my steps. Teach me knowledge and good judgment.

My body is for You, Lord. So here is what I want to do with Your help, Father. I choose to take my everyday, ordinary life—my sleeping, eating, going-to-work, and walking-around life—and place it before You as an offering. Embracing what You do for me is the best thing I can do for You.

Christ (the Messiah) will be magnified and receive glory and praise in this body of mine and will be boldly exalted in my person. Thank You, Father, in Jesus' name! Hallelujah! Amen.

Scripture References

Psalm 139:14 NIV

Romans 12:2 NIV

Jeremiah 29:11 NIV

Proverbs 14:15 NIV

Psalm 119:66 NIV

Romans 12:1 MESSAGE

Philippians 1:20 AMP

To Overcome Fatigue

Introduction

All fatigue does not fall into the category of Chronic Fatigue Syndrome. Most people at one time or another have feelings of apathy and energy loss—times when they go to bed tired and get up tired.

There are cases of fatigue that last for weeks, months, or even years. The medical profession has not determined the causes of Chronic Fatigue Syndrome and does not know its cure. In most individuals it simply runs its course.[4] Where there is no way, Jesus is the Way, the Truth, and the Life (John 14:6). God sent His Word to heal you and deliver you from all your destructions (Ps. 107:20).

According to those who have shared their experience with this syndrome, they have flu-like symptoms—they feel achy with a low-grade fever. One person who suffers from it and for whom we pray is considered disabled and cannot work regularly.

You and I are created triune beings—spirit, soul, and body (1 Thess. 5:23). The apostle John wrote, "Beloved, I wish above all things that thou mayest prosper and be in health, even as thy soul prospereth" (3 John 2).

---

[4] Editors of *Prevention* Magazine, "Symptoms, Their Causes & Cures" (Emmaus, PA: Rodale Press, 1994), pp. 179,181.

God's Word is medicine to our flesh (Prov. 4:20-22 AMP). If any type of medication is to bring relief and a cure, it is necessary to follow the prescribed dosage. This is true with "spiritual" medicine. It is imperative to take doses of God's Word daily through reading, meditating, and listening to healing tapes. The spirit, soul, and body are interrelated; it is the Word of God that brings the entire being into harmony.

God made us and knows us inside and out. He sent His Word to heal us and to deliver us from all our destructions (Ps. 107:20). Prayer prepares us to take action. Jesus said that if we pray in secret, our heavenly Father will reward us openly (Matt. 6:6). Prayer includes praise, worship, and petition.

Prayer prepares us for change—it equips us for action. It puts us in tune and in harmony with the Spirit of God Who is hovering over the face of the rivers of living waters, residing within us (Gen. 1:2; John 7:38). He is waiting for us to speak, to move—to act out our faith. The ministry of the Holy Spirit is revealed in the names ascribed to Him—Comforter, Counselor, Helper, Advocate, Intercessor, Strengthener, Standby (John 16:7 AMP). He is with us and in us (John 14:17).

Prayer

Father, in the name of Jesus, I come before Your throne of grace to receive mercy and to find grace to help in time of need. May blessing (praise, laudation, and eulogy) be to You, the God and Father of my Lord Jesus Christ (the Messiah) for You have blessed me in Christ with every spiritual (given by the Holy Spirit) blessing in the heavenly realm!

Father, Chronic Fatigue Syndrome is a curse, not a blessing. Jesus became a curse, and at the same time dissolved the curse. And now, because of that, the air is cleared, and I can see that Abraham's blessing is present and available for me. I am able to receive Your life, Your Spirit, just the way Abraham received it.

Christ (the Messiah) purchased my freedom with His very own blood, and the law of the Spirit of life [which is] in Christ Jesus [the law of my new being] has freed me from the law of sin and of death.

Christ lives in me. Your Spirit Who raised up Jesus from the dead dwells in me. You, Father, are restoring to life my mortal (short-lived, perishable) body through Your Spirit Who dwells in me.

You, Sovereign Lord, have given me an instructed tongue, to know the word that sustains the weary. You waken me morning by morning, waken my ear to listen like one being taught.

I have strength for all things in Christ Who empowers me [I am ready for anything and equal to anything through

Him Who infuses inner strength into me; I am self-sufficient in Christ's sufficiency].

You are my Light and my Salvation—whom shall I
fear or dread? You are the Refuge and Stronghold of my
life—of whom shall I be afraid? You, Lord, are my Shield,
my Glory, and the Lifter of my head. With my voice I cry
to You, and You hear and answer me out of Your holy hill.
I lie down and sleep; I awaken again, and You sustain me.

Father, I put on Your whole armor; and, having done
all, I stand, knowing that You are watching over Your
Word to perform it. Your Word will not return to You
void [without producing any effect, useless], but it shall
accomplish that which You please and purpose, and it
shall prosper in the thing for which You sent it.

Lord, You used Your servant body to carry my sins to
the cross so I could be rid of sin, free to live the right way.
Your wounds became my healing.

I throw off the spirit of heaviness and exchange it for a
garment of praise. Thank You for the superhuman energy
which You so mightily enkindle and work within me.

In the name of Jesus I pray, amen.

Scripture References

Hebrews 4:16

Ephesians 1:3 AMP

Galatians 3:13,14 MESSAGE

Acts 20:28

Romans 8:2,11 AMP

Isaiah 50:4 NIV

Philippians 4:13 AMP

Psalm 27:1 AMP

Psalm 3:3-5 AMP

Ephesians 6:11,13

Jeremiah 1:12 AMP

Isaiah 55:11 AMP

1 Peter 2:24 MESSAGE

Isaiah 61:3

Colossians 1:29 AMP

To Bear Fruit

Lord Jesus, You chose me and appointed me to go and bear fruit—fruit that will last. Then the Father will give me whatever I ask in Your name. Father, You are the Gardener. You prune every branch that bears fruit, so it will be even more fruitful.

The apostle Paul said that we are to be filled with the fruit of righteousness and that he desired that fruit might abound to our account. Therefore, I commit myself to bring forth the fruit of the spirit: love, joy, peace, longsuffering, gentleness, goodness, faith, meekness, and temperance. I renounce and turn from the fruit of the flesh, because I belong to Christ and have crucified the flesh with its affections and lusts.

A seed cannot bear fruit unless it first falls into the ground and dies. I confess that I am crucified with Christ: nevertheless I live; yet not I, but Christ lives in me. And the life that I now live in the flesh I live by the faith of the Son of God, Who loved me and gave Himself for me.

Father, I thank You that I am good ground, that I hear Your Word and understand it, and that the Word bears fruit in my life—sometimes a hundredfold, sometimes sixty, sometimes thirty. I am like a tree planted by the rivers of water that brings forth fruit in its season. My leaf shall not wither, and whatever I do shall prosper.

Father, in Jesus' name, I thank You for filling me with the knowledge of Your will in all wisdom and spiritual understanding that I may walk worthy of You, Lord, being fruitful in every good work and increasing in the knowledge of You. Amen.

Scripture References

John 15:16 NIV	Galatians 2:20
John 15:1,2 NIV	Matthew 13:23
Philippians 1:11	Psalm 1:3
Philippians 4:17	Colossians 1:9,10
Galatians 5:22-24	John 12:24

Godly Wisdom in the Affairs of Life

Father, You said that if anyone lacks wisdom, let him ask of You, Who gives to all men liberally and upbraids not; and it shall be given him. Therefore, I ask in faith, nothing wavering, to be filled with the knowledge of Your will in all wisdom and spiritual understanding. Today I incline my ear unto wisdom, and I apply my heart to understanding so that I might receive that which has been freely given unto me.

In the name of Jesus, I receive skillful and godly wisdom and instruction. I discern and comprehend the words of understanding and insight. I receive instruction in wise dealing and the discipline of wise thoughtfulness, righteousness, justice, and integrity. Prudence, knowledge, discretion, and discernment are given to me. I increase in knowledge. As a person of understanding, I acquire skill and attain to sound counsel [so that I may be able to steer my course rightly].

Wisdom will keep, defend, and protect me; I love her, and she guards me. I prize wisdom highly and exalt her; she will bring me to honor because I embrace her. She gives to my head a wreath of gracefulness; a crown of beauty and glory will she deliver to me. Length of days is in her right hand, and in her left hand are riches and honor.

Jesus has been made unto me wisdom, and in Him are all the treasures of [divine] wisdom, of comprehensive insight into Your ways and purposes, and in Him [all the riches of spiritual] knowledge and enlightenment are stored up and lie hidden. Lord, You have hidden away sound and godly wisdom and stored it up for me, for I am Your righteousness in Christ Jesus.

Therefore, I will walk in paths of uprightness. When I walk, my steps shall not be hampered—my path will be clear and open; and when I run, I shall not stumble. I take firm hold of instruction and do not let her go; I guard her, for she is my life. I let my eyes look right on [with fixed purpose], and my gaze is straight before me. I consider well the path of my feet, and I let all my ways be established and ordered aright.

Father, in the name of Jesus, I look carefully to how I walk! I live purposefully and worthily and accurately, not as unwise and witless, but as a wise—sensible, intelligent—person, making the very most of my time [buying up each opportunity]. Amen.

Scripture References

James 1:5,6	1 Corinthians 1:30
Colossians 1:9	Colossians 2:3 AMP
Proverbs 2:2 AMP	Proverbs 2:7 AMP
Proverbs 1:2-5 AMP	2 Corinthians 5:21
Proverbs 4:6,8,9 AMP	Proverbs 4:11-13,25,26 AMP
Proverbs 3:16 AMP	Ephesians 5:15,16 AMP

To Receive a Discerning Heart

Father, I thank You for creating within me a wise and discerning heart, so that I am able to distinguish between right and wrong.

This is my prayer: that my love may abound more and more in knowledge and depth of insight, so that I may be able to discern what is best and may be pure and blameless until the day of Christ, filled with the fruit of righteousness that comes through Jesus Christ—to Your glory and praise, O Lord.

Father, I trust in You with all my heart and lean not on my own understanding; in all my ways I acknowledge You, and You will make my paths straight. Through Your precepts I get understanding; therefore, I hate every false way. Your Word is a lamp to my feet and a light to my path.

Joseph, in Genesis 41:39-41 NIV, was described as a discerning and wise man who was put in charge of the entire land of Egypt. As You were with Joseph, Moses, and other strong, godly men and women in the Bible, so shall You be with me. You will cause me to find favor at my place of employment, at home, or wherever I may be.

I make [special] request, [asking] that I may be filled with the full (deep and clear) knowledge of Your will in all spiritual wisdom and in understanding and discernment of spiritual things—that I may walk (live and conduct myself) in a manner worthy of You, Lord, fully pleasing to You and desiring to please You in all things, steadily growing and increasing in and by Your knowledge [with fuller, deeper, and clearer insight, acquaintance, and recognition].

Because Jesus has been made unto me wisdom, I listen and add to my learning; I discern and get guidance, understanding what Your will is.

In the name of Jesus I pray, amen.

Scripture References

1 Kings 3:9 NIV   Proverbs 3:1-4

Philippians 1:9-11 NIV   Colossians 1:9,10 AMP

Proverbs 3:5 NIV   1 Corinthians 1:30

Psalm 119:104,105 AMP   Proverbs 1:5

Genesis 41:39-41 NIV   Ephesians 5:17 NIV

Joshua 1:5

Overcoming the Day of Trouble

Introduction

During a time of trouble or calamity, it is sometimes difficult to remember the promises of God. The pressures of the moment may seem overwhelming. At such times, it is often helpful to read, meditate on, and pray the entire chapter of Psalm 91.

It may be that during a stressful time you will find this entire prayer too long. If so, draw from the Scriptures included in the following prayer. You may find yourself praying one paragraph or reading it aloud to yourself or to your family and friends.

I also encourage you to meditate on this prayer during good times.

At all times, remember that faith comes by hearing, and hearing by the Word of God (Rom. 10:17).

Prayer

Father, I come to You in the name of Jesus, acknowledging You as my Refuge and High Tower. You are a refuge and a stronghold in these times of trouble (high cost, destitution, and desperation).

In the day of trouble You will hide me in Your shelter; in the secret place of Your tent will You hide me; You will set me high upon a rock. And now shall my head be lifted up above my enemies round about me; in Your tent I will offer sacrifices and shouting of joy; I will sing, yes, I will sing praises to You, O Lord. Hear, O Lord, when I cry aloud; have mercy and be gracious to me and answer me!

On the authority of Your Word, I declare that I have been made the righteousness of God in Christ Jesus. When I cry for help, You, Lord, hear me and deliver me out of all my distress and troubles. You are close to me, for I am of a broken heart, and You save such who are crushed with sorrow for sin and are humbly and thoroughly penitent. Lord, many are the evils that confront me, but You deliver me out of them all.

Thank You for being merciful and gracious to me, O God, for my soul takes refuge and finds shelter and confidence in You; yes, in the shadow of Your wings I take refuge and am confident until calamities and destructive storms are past. You perform on my behalf and reward me. You bring to pass Your purposes for me, and surely You complete them!

Father, You are my Refuge and Strength [mighty and impenetrable to temptation], a very present and well-proved help in trouble.

Lord, You have given and bequeathed to me Your peace. By Your grace, I will not let my heart be troubled, neither will I let it be afraid. With the help of the Holy Spirit, I will [stop allowing myself to be agitated and disturbed; and I refuse to permit myself to be fearful and intimidated and cowardly and unsettled].

By faith, I respond to these troubles and calamities: [I am full of joy now!] I exult and triumph in my troubles and rejoice in my sufferings, knowing that pressure and affliction and hardship produce patient and unswerving endurance. And endurance (fortitude) develops maturity of character (approved faith and tried integrity). And character [of this sort] produces [the habit of] joyful and confident hope of eternal salvation. Such hope never disappoints or deludes or shames me, for Your love has been poured out in my heart through the Holy Spirit Who has been given to me.

In Jesus' name, amen.

Scripture References

Psalm 9:9 AMP	Psalm 57:1,2 AMP
Psalm 27:5-7 AMP	Psalm 46:1 AMP
2 Corinthians 5:21	John 14:27 AMP
Psalm 34:17-20 AMP	Romans 5:3-5 AMP

For Victory in Court Cases

Father, in the name of Jesus, it is written in Your Word to call on You, and You will answer me and show me great and mighty things. I put You in remembrance of Your Word and thank You that You watch over it to perform it.

I say that no weapon formed against me shall prosper, and any tongue that rises against me in judgment I shall show to be in the wrong. This peace, righteousness, security, and triumph over opposition is my inheritance as Your child. This is the righteousness or vindication I obtain from You, Father, which You impart to me as my justification. I am far from even the thought of destruction; for I shall not fear, and terror shall not come near me.

Father, You say You will establish me to the end—keep me steadfast, give me strength, and guarantee my vindication; that is, be my warrant against all accusation or indictment. Father, You contend with those who contend with me, and You perfect that which concerns me. I dwell in the secret place of the Most High, and this secret place hides me from the strife of tongues, for a false witness who breathes out lies is an abomination to You.

I am a true witness, and all my words are (upright and in right standing with You), Father. My long forbearing and calmness of spirit persuade the judge, and my soft speech breaks down the most bone-like resistance.

Therefore, I am not anxious [beforehand] how I shall reply in defense or what I am to say, for the Holy Spirit will teach me *in that very hour* and moment what [I] ought to say to those in the outside world. My speech is seasoned with salt.

As a child of the light, I enforce the triumphant victory of my Lord Jesus Christ in this situation, knowing that all of heaven is backing me. I am strong in You, Lord, and in the power of Your might. Thank You for the shield of faith that quenches every fiery dart of the enemy. I am increasing in wisdom and in stature and in years, and in favor with You, Father, and with man. Praise the Lord! Amen.

Scripture References

Jeremiah 33:3	Proverbs 6:17,19 AMP
Isaiah 43:26 AMP	Proverbs 14:25
Jeremiah 1:12 AMP	Proverbs 8:8 AMP
Isaiah 54:17 AMP	Proverbs 25:15 AMP
Isaiah 54:14 AMP	Luke 12:11,12 AMP
1 Corinthians 1:8 AMP	Colossians 4:6
Isaiah 49:25	Matthew 18:18
Psalm 138:8	Ephesians 6:10,16
Psalm 91:1	Luke 2:52 AMP
Psalm 31:20	

Resting in the Lord

Jesus, I am weary and burdened, and I come to You, knowing that You will give me rest. I take Your yoke upon me and learn from You, for You are gentle and humble in heart, and I will find rest for my soul. Your yoke is easy, and Your burden is light.

In the name of Jesus, I will praise You, my Lord, Who counsels me; even at night my heart instructs me. Lord, I have set You always before me. Because You are at my right hand, I will not be shaken. Therefore, my heart is glad and my tongue rejoices; my body also will rest secure, because You will not abandon me. You have made known to me the path of life; You fill me with joy in Your presence, with eternal pleasures at Your right hand.

Lord God, my soul finds rest in You alone; my salvation comes from You. You alone are my Rock and my Salvation; because You are my Fortress, I will never be shaken. My soul finds rest in You alone; my hope comes from You. My salvation and my honor depend on You; You are my mighty Rock, my Refuge. I trust in You at all times; I pour out my heart to You, my God, because You are my Refuge.

In repentance and rest is my salvation, in quietness and trust is my strength. My soul is at rest, O Lord, because You have been good to me. I dwell in the shelter of the Most High, resting in the shadow of the Almighty.

In Jesus' name. Amen.

Scripture References

Matthew 11:28-30 NIV   Isaiah 30:15 NIV

Psalm 16:7-11 NIV   Psalm 116:7 NIV

Psalm 62:1,2,5,7,8 NIV   Psalm 91:1 NIV

Part III

Prayers for Financial Increase/Provision

God Is Your Provider

Father God, You are my Provider, and You will provide a place for me and will plant me so that I can have a home of my own and no longer be disturbed. You will also give me rest from all my enemies. You provide food for those who fear You, and You have shown me the power of Your works. The works of Your hands are faithful and just; all Your precepts are trustworthy. They are steadfast forever and ever, done in faithfulness and uprightness. You have provided redemption for Your people; You have ordained Your covenant forever—holy and awesome is Your name.

I purpose to forget the former things; I will not dwell on the past, and it will no longer control my decisions. I see that You are doing a new thing! I perceive that it is now springing up. O my Father, You provide water in the desert and streams in the wasteland, to give me drink. I am Your chosen; You formed me for Yourself that I may proclaim Your praise. I thank You for bringing health and healing to me, and allowing me to enjoy abundant peace and security. You brought me out of captivity, and You are helping me rebuild my life.

In the name of Jesus I confess my sin of rebellion against You, and I thank You for Your forgiveness—You are cleansing me from all unrighteousness. The people will praise and honor You before all nations on earth as they hear of all the good things You do for me. The people will be in awe and will tremble at the abundant prosperity and peace You have provided for me.

Father, You have supplied me with seed that I may sow, and have given me bread for food. You will also supply and increase my store of seed and will enlarge the harvest of my righteousness. I pray that You will make my love increase and overflow for others. Lord, the God of my fathers, increase me a thousand times and bless me as You have promised! I shall prosper and be in health, even as my soul prospers, in the name of Jesus. Amen.

Scripture References

2 Samuel 7:10,11 NIV   1 John 1:9

Psalm 111:5-9 NIV   2 Corinthians 9:10 NIV

Isaiah 43:18-21 NIV   1 Thessalonians 3:12 NIV

Jeremiah 33:6-9 NIV   Deuteronomy 1:11

3 John 2

For God's Supply of Your Every Need

God, I come before Your throne of grace where I receive mercy and find grace to help me in my time of need. Father, I know that You are able to make all grace abound to me, so that in all things at all times, having all that I need, I will abound in every good work. As it is written: "He has scattered abroad his gifts to the poor; his righteousness endures forever" (2 Cor. 9:9 NIV). You supply seed to the sower and bread for food, and I trust You to also supply and increase my store of seed and enlarge the harvest of my righteousness. I will be made rich in every way so that I can be generous on every occasion.

I have learned the secret of being content in any and every situation, whether well fed or hungry, whether living in plenty or in want. I can do everything through Christ Who gives me strength. Father, I thank You for meeting all my needs according to Your glorious riches in Christ Jesus.

Night and day I pray most earnestly that You, Lord, will supply what is lacking in my faith, and make my love increase and overflow for everyone. I purpose to share with Your people who are in need, and to practice hospitality. In my season of plenty I will supply what others need, so that in turn their plenty will supply what I need. Then there will be equality, as it is written: "He who gathered much did not have too much, and he who gathered little did not have too little" (2 Cor. 8:15 NIV).

Your divine power has given me everything I need for life and godliness through my knowledge of You Who called me by Your own glory and goodness. I pray that these words of mine, which I have prayed before You, will be near to You day and night, that You may uphold my cause according to each day's need.

In Jesus' name I pray, amen.

Scripture References

Hebrews 4:16 NIV

Romans 12:13 NIV

2 Corinthians 9:8-11 NIV

2 Corinthians 8:14,15 NIV

Philippians 4:12,13,19 NIV

2 Peter 1:3 NIV

1 Thessalonians 3:10-12 NIV

1 Kings 8:59 NIV

Dedication of Your Tithes

I profess this day unto You, Lord God, that I have come into the inheritance which You swore to give me. I am in the land, which You have provided for me in Jesus Christ, Your Kingdom, Almighty God. I was a sinner serving Satan; he was my god. But I called upon the name of Jesus, and You heard my cry and delivered me into the Kingdom of Your dear Son.

Jesus, as my Lord and High Priest, I bring the first-fruits of my income to You and worship You with it.

I rejoice in all the good that You have given to me and my household. I have hearkened to Your voice, Lord God, and have done according to all that You have commanded me. Now look down from Your holy habitation, from heaven, and bless me as You have said in Your Word. I thank You, Father, in Jesus' name, amen.

Scripture References

Deuteronomy 26:1,3,10,11,14,15 AMP   Colossians 1:13

Ephesians 2:1-5   Hebrews 3:1,7,8

To Give Your Finances to the Lord

Father, in the name of Jesus, I repent for the times I have robbed You of tithes and offerings. I have depended on my own strength to acquire financial security, but I am not sufficient of myself to think any thing as of myself; but my sufficiency is of You.

Forgive me for speaking against You, and for withholding blessings from others. I approach You with clean hands and a pure heart to seek Your will. There are so many ministries and people in financial need; I am asking You to direct me in my giving. You have brought me out of the darkness of bondage into Your marvelous light, and the blood of Your Son, Jesus, redeems me. I bring my whole tithe into Your storehouse that there may be food in Your house, trusting Your Word that You will open the floodgates of heaven and pour out so much blessing on me that I will not have room enough for it.

When I give my offerings to benefit Your people and increase Your Kingdom, I will remember that I am bringing my offerings to You even as my heart prompts me. My giving shall be done with simplicity.

In the name of Jesus, I renounce, smash, and annihilate the need to impress others or to buy their love and acceptance, because I am accepted in the Beloved. I bind my mind to the mind of Christ, my emotions to the control of the Holy Spirit, and will give my offerings as the Holy Spirit directs me. I purpose to give what I have decided in my heart to give, not reluctantly or under compulsion. I am a cheerful giver. And Lord, You are able to make all grace abound to me, so that in all things at all times, having all that I need, I will abound in every good work. In love and in obedience to Your will, I give tithes and offerings out of that which You have entrusted to my stewardship.

As a child imitates the father, I will follow You; walking in love, in the light (in all goodness, righteousness, and truth) and walking circumspectly, not as a fool, but as a wise person, understanding Your will for my life. All that I have is Yours, and I will no longer withhold good from those who deserve it, when it is in my power to act, but will give in the blessed name of my Lord and Savior, Jesus Christ. Amen.

Scripture References

Malachi 3:8,13,14 NIV

2 Corinthians 3:5

Psalm 24:3,4 NIV

1 Peter 2:9

1 Peter 1:18,19

Malachi 3:10 NIV

Exodus 25:2 NIV

Romans 12:8

Ephesians 1:6

Matthew 18:18

1 Corinthians 2:16

James 4:7

2 Corinthians 9:7,8 NIV

Ephesians 5:1,2,8,9,15,17

Proverbs 3:27 NIV

Prosperity

Father, I come to You in the name of Jesus concerning my financial situation. You are a very present help in trouble, and You are more than enough. Your Word declares that You shall supply all my need according to Your riches in glory by Christ Jesus.

(If you have not been giving tithes and offerings, include this statement of repentance in your prayer.) Forgive me for robbing You in tithes and offerings. I repent and purpose to bring all my tithes into the storehouse that there may be food in Your house. Thank You for wise financial counselors and teachers who are teaching me the principles of good stewardship.

Lord of hosts, You said, "Try Me now in this... If I will not open for you the windows of heaven and pour out for you such blessing that there will not be room enough to receive it" (Mal. 3:10 NKJV). You will rebuke the devourer for my sake, and my heart is filled with thanksgiving.

Lord, my God, I shall remember that it is You Who give me the power to get wealth, that You may establish Your covenant. In the name of Jesus, I worship You, and You only, and I will have no other gods before me.

You are able to make all grace (every favor and earthly blessing) come to me in abundance, so that I am always, and in all circumstances, furnished in abundance for every good work and charitable donation. Amen.

Scripture References

Psalm 56:1

Psalm 4:6 MESSAGE

Philippians 4:19

Malachi 3:8-12

Deuteronomy 8:18,19

Exodus 20:3

Luke 4:8

2 Corinthians 9:8 AMP

Success in Business

Father, Your Word says that I am a partaker of the inheritance and treasures of heaven. You have delivered me out of
the authority of darkness and translated me into the Kingdom
of Your dear Son. Father, where Your Word is there is light
and, also, understanding. Your Word does not return to You
void but always accomplishes what it is sent to do. I am a
joint-heir with Jesus; and as Your son/daughter, I accept that
the communication of my faith is effectual by the acknowledging of every good work that is in me in Christ Jesus.

Father, I commit my works (the plans and cares of my
business) to You, entrusting them wholly to You. Since You
are effectually at work in me, You cause my thoughts to
become agreeable with Your will, so that my business plans
shall be established and succeed. In the name of Jesus, I
submit to every kind of wisdom, practical insight, and
prudence, which You have lavished upon me in accordance
with the riches and generosity of Your gracious favor.

Father, I affirm that I obey Your Word by making an
honest living with my own hands, so that I may be able to
give to those in need. In Your strength and according to
Your grace, I provide for myself and my own family.
Thank You, Father, for making all grace (every favor and
earthly blessing) come to me in abundance so that I,
having all sufficiency, may abound to every good work.

Father, thank You for the ministering spirits that You have assigned to go forth to bring in clients. Jesus said to His disciples, "You are the light of the world" (Matt. 5:14 AMP). In His name my light shall so shine before all men that they may see my good works glorifying You, my heavenly Father.

Thank You for the grace to remain diligent in seeking knowledge and skill in areas where I am inexperienced. I ask You for wisdom and the ability to understand righteousness, justice, and fair dealing [in every area and relationship]. I affirm that I am faithful and committed to Your Word. My life and business are founded upon its principles.

Father, thank You for the success of my business!

In Your name, amen.

Scripture References

Romans 8:17 NLT	Ephesians 4:28
Colossians 1:12,13	1 Timothy 5:8 AMP
Psalm 119:130	2 Corinthians 9:8 AMP
Isaiah 55:11	Hebrews 1:14 AMP
Philemon 1:6	Matthew 5:14,16 AMP
Proverbs 16:3	Proverbs 22:29 AMP
Philippians 2:13	Proverbs 2:9
Ephesians 1:7,8 AMP	Proverbs 4:20-22

Employment

Father, in Jesus' name, I believe and confess Your Word today, knowing that You watch over it to perform it. Your Word prospers whereto it is sent! Father, You are my [Source] of every comfort (consolation and encouragement). As a result, I am courageous and grow in strength.

My desire is to owe no man anything, except to love him. Therefore, I am strong, and I will not let my hands be weak or slack, for my work shall be rewarded. My wages are not counted as a favor or a gift, but as an obligation (something owed to me). I make it my ambition and definitely endeavor to live quietly and peacefully, mind my own affairs, and work with my own hands. I am correct and honorable and command the respect of the outside world, being self-supporting, dependent on nobody, and having need of nothing; for You, Father, supply to the full my every need.

I work in quietness, earning my own food and other necessities. I am not weary of doing right, (but I continue in well-doing without weakening). I learn to apply myself to good deeds [to honest labor and honorable employment] so that I am able to meet necessary demands whenever the occasion may require.

Father, You know [the record of] my works and what I am doing. You have set before me a door wide open, which no one is able to shut.

Therefore, I do not fear, and I am not dismayed, for You, Father, strengthen me. You, Father, help me in Jesus' name; in Jesus, I have perfect peace and confidence and am of good cheer, for Jesus has overcome the world and [deprived it of its power to harm me]. I do not fret or have anxiety about anything, for Your peace, Father, mounts guard over my heart and mind. I know the secret of facing every situation, for I am self-sufficient in Christ's sufficiency. I guard my mouth and my tongue, keeping myself from trouble.

I prize Your wisdom, Father, and acknowledge You. You direct, make straight and plain, my path, and You promote me. Therefore, Father, I increase in Your wisdom (in broad and full understanding) and in stature and years and in favor with You, Father, and with man! Amen.

Scripture References

Jeremiah 1:12 AMP

Isaiah 55:11

2 Corinthians 1:3 AMP

1 Corinthians 16:13 AMP

Romans 13:8 AMP

2 Chronicles 15:7 AMP

Romans 4:4 AMP

1 Thessalonians 4:11,12 AMP

2 Thessalonians 3:12,13 AMP

Titus 3:14 AMP

Revelation 3:8 AMP

Isaiah 41:10 AMP

John 16:33 AMP

Philippians 4:6,7 AMP

Philippians 4:12,13 AMP

Proverbs 21:23 AMP

Proverbs 4:8 AMP

Proverbs 3:6 AMP

Luke 2:52 AMP

For Wisdom in Daily Financial Decisions*

Father, I know that it is Your will that I prosper financially even as my soul prospers. In the name of Jesus, I bind my mind to the mind of Christ, my financial decisions to the will of God, and my emotions to the control of the Holy Spirit. I resist the temptation to be slothful in business, and I purpose to be prompt about fulfilling my responsibilities with fervency of spirit, serving You. I pray that my integrity and uprightness will protect me, because my hope is in You.

It is my desire to go out into the world uncorrupted, a breath of fresh air in this squalid and polluted society, and to provide people with a glimpse of good living and of the living God. That's why I pay my taxes, my bills, and respect my leaders. I resist the temptation to run up debts; except for the huge debt of love I owe others.

It is my ambition to lead a quiet life, to mind my own business, and to work with my own hands. I will study to show myself approved in finances and will attend diligently to my financial responsibilities. Jesus is made unto me wisdom, and I thank You, Father, for getting godly information—books, tapes, teaching seminars—to me so that I can make wise financial decisions. The slothful person craves and gets nothing, but the desires of the diligent are fully satisfied. In the name of Jesus I will be a living witness and a good steward of all that You have given me. Amen.

Scripture References

3 John 2

Matthew 18:18

1 Corinthians 2:16

James 4:7

2 Corinthians 9:7,8 NIV

James 4:7

Romans 12:11

Psalm 119:24

Psalm 25:21 NIV

Philipians 2:15 MESSAGE

Romans 13:6-8 MESSAGE

1 Thes. 4:11 NIV

2 Timothy 2:15 NIV

1 Corinthians 1:30

Proverbs 6:6 NIV

Proverbs 13:4 NIV

Acts 1:8

1 Corinthians 4:2

---

* To acquire wisdom in daily financial decisions, I recommend reading the book of Proverbs. There are many Bible-based books to help you learn God's principles of tithing, giving, saving, and budgeting.

Handling Household Finances

Introduction

The following prayers may be prayed individually (as a single person) or as a single parent heading a single parent household. Financial problems are one of Satan's greatest weapons for introducing strife and bringing pressure to bear on individuals. Mismanaging finances and spending money can quickly evolve into an emotional experience, causing many other problems.

God is *El-Shaddai*, God Almighty (Ex. 6:3 AMP)—the God Who is more than enough (Ps. 4:6 MESSAGE)—and His intention is that His children enjoy good health and that all may go well with them, even as their souls are getting along well (3 John 2 NIV). Coming into agreement with God's financial plan will offset the enemy's schemes to steal, kill, and destroy (John 10:10) your prosperity and your faith.

If you are planning to establish a financial plan in your home, listen to the leading of the Holy Spirit in your heart. Understand what the Word says about finances (Ps. 119:24). Determine to be astute in financial matters: balancing the checkbook, paying the bills on time, and making wise investments. Set aside time in your schedule to review goals and make financial plans. Wisdom from above is willing to yield to reason (James 3:17 AMP).

God's ways are not our ways; His thoughts are higher than our thoughts. In other words, the way God works surpasses the way that we work, and the way He thinks is beyond the way that we think (Isa. 55:8,9 MESSAGE)—and His thoughts and ways are always the best.

Prayer

Father, I come before You in the name of Jesus. Thank You for the Holy Spirit Who is present with me to help me with my financial future. Thank You for bringing me to this place in my life. You have started a good work in me and will perform it until the day of Christ. I welcome You as I prepare to set up a budget that is pleasing to You and myself.

Jesus, You are my Lord and my High Priest, and I purpose to bring You the firstfruits of my income and worship You, the Lord my God, with them.

Father, You are Lord over my life—over this home that I believe has been ordained by You. I confess Your Word over my life and my finances. As I do so, I say that Your Word will not return to You void, but will accomplish what You send it to do.

Therefore, I believe, in the name of Jesus, that all of my needs are met, according to Your riches in glory. I acknowledge You as Lord over my finances by giving tithes and offerings to further Your cause.

Father, on the authority of Your Word, I declare that gifts will be given unto me; good measure, pressed down, shaken together, and running over shall they be poured into my bosom. For with the same measure I deal out, it shall be measured back to me.

I remember that it is written in Your Word that he who sows sparingly and grudgingly will also reap sparingly and grudgingly, and he who sows generously [that blessings may come to someone] will also reap generously and with blessings.

Lord, remind me always, and I purpose to remember, that it is You Who gives me power to become rich, and You do it to fulfill Your promise to my ancestors. I will never feel that it was my own power and might that made me wealthy.

Father, not only do I give tithes and offerings to You, but I also give to those around me who are in need. Your Word also says that he who gives to the poor lends to You, and You pay wonderful interest on the loan! I acknowledge You as I give for the benefit of the poor.

Thank You, Father, that as You bless me and I bless others, they will praise You and give You thanks and bless others, and the circle of Your love and blessing will go on and on into eternity.

In the name of Jesus we pray, amen.

Scripture References

John 14:17	Luke 6:38
Philippians 1:6	2 Corinthians 9:6 AMP
Hebrews 3:1	Deuteronomy 8:17,18 TLB
Deuteronomy 26:10,11	Proverbs 19:17 TLB
Isaiah 55:11	2 Corinthians 9:12-15
Philippians 4:19	AMP, NIV, PHILLIPS

I.

Setting Aside the Tithe

Father, Your Word states, "Be sure to set aside a tenth of all that your fields produce each year....so that you may learn to revere the LORD your God always" (Deut. 14:22,23 NIV). I purpose to set aside the tithe because it belongs to You, O God our Father.

It is my delight to bring all the tithes (the whole tenth of my income) into the storehouse, that there may be food in Your house. Lord of hosts, in accordance with Your Word, I prove You now by paying You the tithe. You are opening the windows of heaven for me and pouring me out a blessing, that there shall not be room enough to receive it.

Thank You, Father, for rebuking the devourer for my sake; he shall not destroy the fruits of my ground, neither shall my vine drop its fruit before the time in the field.

I praise You, Lord, for recording my name in Your book of remembrance of those who reverence and worshipfully fear You and who think on Your name so that we may be Yours in the day when You publicly recognize and openly declare us to be Your jewels (Your special possession, Your peculiar treasure).

Thank You for bringing me out of the authority of darkness and translating me into the Kingdom of Your dear Son, Jesus Christ, my Lord.

In His name I pray, amen.

Scripture References

Malachi 3:10,11 AMP   Colossians 1:13 NIV
Malachi 3:16,17 AMP

II.

Giving the Offering

Father, I give offerings at the direction of the Holy Spirit. I am ever ready with a generous and willing gift. At Your instructions I [remember] this: He who sows sparingly and grudgingly will also reap sparingly and grudgingly, and he who sows generously [that blessings may come to someone] will also reap generously and with blessings.

I [give] as I make up my own mind and purpose in my heart, not reluctantly or sorrowfully or under compulsion;

for You, Lord, love (take pleasure in, prize above other things, and are unwilling to abandon or to do without) a cheerful (joyous "prompt to do it") giver [whose heart is in his giving].

Father, I thank You that You are able to make all grace (every favor and earthly blessing) come to me in abundance, so that I may always, under all circumstances and whatever the need, be self-sufficient [possessing enough to require no aid or support and furnished in abundance for every good work and charitable donation].

Father, [You] provide seed for my sowing and bread for my eating. Thank You for providing and multiplying [my resources for] sowing and increasing the fruits of my righteousness. Thus I will be enriched in all things and in every way, so that I can be generous, and [my generosity as it is] administered by me will bring forth thanksgiving to You.

I confess with the psalmist David, I have not seen the righteous forsaken, nor his seed begging bread.

Thank You for my food, clothing, and shelter. In the name of Jesus, I determine to stop being perpetually uneasy (anxious and worried) about my life as a single person, what I shall eat and what I shall drink, or about my body, what I shall put on. My life is greater [in quality] than food, and my body [far above and more excellent] than clothing.

The bread of idleness [gossip, discontent, and self-pity] I will not eat. I declare on the authority of Your Word that I will be mighty in the land: this generation of the upright will be blessed.

Father, You delight in the prosperity of Your people; thank You that wealth and riches are in my house and that my righteousness endures forever.

Good comes to me for I am generous and lend freely and conduct my affairs with justice. When I lack wisdom, I will ask of You, and You will give generously without finding fault with me.

In the name of Jesus, amen.

Scripture References

2 Corinthians 9:5-11 AMP	Psalm 112:2,3 NIV
Psalm 37:25	Psalm 37:26 NIV
Matthew 6:25 AMP	2 Corinthians 9:10 AMP
Proverbs 31:27 AMP	James 1:5 NIV
Psalm 35:27	

Facing Financial Crisis

Lord, I come to You in this time of great need in my life. Whatever the cause, I find myself in extreme financial need.

First of all, Father, I come against the spirit of fear, in the name of Jesus. I refuse to operate in fear, anxiety, or worry concerning this situation. I know it is serious, and I do not approach it flippantly. But I know that if there is fear, anxiety, or worry in my heart, it will cloud my judgment and appraisal of the situation. It will make it seem even worse than it really is. It will also block my ability to hear from You.

Father, I give this whole situation to You and ask for Your guidance and direction in rectifying it. If it came about because of any bad decisions I made or any wrong thoughts or actions I engaged in, I repent to You right now. I ask You for forgiveness. Help me to see my mistakes and faults and to do all in my power to overcome and correct them.

Lord, if this financial crisis is the result of my negligence or my irresponsible spending, I ask You to forgive me. Help me to be sensitive to Your voice so that I may hear from You as I seek Your counsel. I open my heart to You. Show me what to do so that such a crisis as this one never occurs again.

Concerning the current need, I ask You to help me and to give me favor with those to whom I owe money. I thank You for an increase in income so my financial resources can grow, knowledge so I will know where to cut expenses, and insight so I will know how to budget the money that I do have.

Thank You for supernatural wisdom so I can see how to walk out of this terrible situation. Help me to formulate a plan of recovery, a plan to get from where I am today to where I want to be tomorrow. Help me to communicate that plan clearly and effectively to my family, friends, and loved ones who will be involved in it or affected by it.

Lord, send me counselors, those who can help me with this task. Send me people with wisdom and insight concerning this situation, so that they might help me perceive and discern Your perfect plan for recovery.

Father, I give myself entirely to You. Thank You that I hear Your voice accurately and distinctly as You reveal to me what to do and how to do it. I ask You to help me identify the reason I got into this crisis in the first place and to erect safeguards so that it will never happen again.

Thank You for Your forgiveness, Your help, Your wisdom, and Your instruction. Thank You that I am totally and completely out of this crisis. I receive it by faith and thank You that it is done, in Jesus' name. Amen.

Scripture References

2 Timothy 1:7

Philippians 4:6 AMP

Ephesians 5:17

John 10:27 NIV

Psalm 5:12

Psalm 115:14

Daniel 2:21-23 AMP

Acts 6:10

Psalm 1:1

Psalm 16:7 AMP

Psalm 73:24

Proverbs 15:22 NIV

Job 22:28

Part IV

Prayers
for Your
Relationships

For Your Family Members

Father, in the name of Jesus, I thank You that You have poured Your Spirit upon our family from on high. Our wilderness has become a fruitful field, and we value our fruitful field as a forest. Justice dwells in our wilderness, and righteousness [moral and spiritual rectitude in every area and relation] abides in our fruitful field. The effect of righteousness will be peace [internal and external], and the result of righteousness will be quietness and confident trust forever.

Our family dwells in a peaceable habitation, in safe dwellings, and in quiet resting places. And there is stability in our times, abundance of salvation, wisdom, and knowledge. There, reverent fear and worship of You, Lord, is our treasure and Yours.

O Lord, be gracious to us; we have waited [expectantly] for You. Be the [Arm of Your servants—our Strength and Defense] every morning, our Salvation in the time of trouble.

Father, we thank You for our salvation, wisdom, and knowledge, and for our peace, safety, and welfare this day. Amen.

Scripture References

Isaiah 32:15-18 AMP   Isaiah 33:2,6 AMP

To Choose Godly Friends

Father, help me to meet new friends—friends who will encourage me. May I find in these friendships the companionship and fellowship You have ordained for me. I know that You are my Source of love, companionship, and friendship. Your love and friendship are expressed through my relationship with You and members of the Body of Christ.

According to Proverbs 27:17 CEV, as iron sharpens iron, so friends sharpen the minds of each other. As we learn from each other, may we find a worthy purpose in our relationship. Keep me well-balanced in my friendships, so that I will always please You rather than pleasing other people.

I ask for divine connections—good friendships ordained by You. Thank You for the courage and grace to let go of detrimental friendships. I ask and receive, by faith, discernment for developing healthy relationships. Your Word says that two are better than one, because if one falls, there will be someone to lift that person up.

Father, You know the hearts of people, so I won't be deceived by outward appearances. Bad friendships corrupt good morals. Thank You for quality friends who help me build a stronger character and draw me closer to You. Help me be a friend to others and to love my friends at all times.

I will laugh with those who laugh, I will rejoice with those who rejoice, and I will weep with those who weep. Teach me what I need to know to be a quality friend.

Develop in me a fun personality and a good sense of humor. Help me to relax around people and to be myself—the person You created me to be. Instruct my heart and mold my character, that I may be faithful and trustworthy over the friendships You are sending into my life.

Father, Your Son, Jesus, is my best Friend. He is a Friend Who sticks closer than a brother. He defined the standard when He said in John 15:13, "Greater love hath no man than this, that a man lay down his life for his friends."

Thank You, Lord, that I can entrust myself and my need for friends into Your keeping. I submit to the leadership of the Holy Spirit, in the name of Jesus. Amen.

Scripture References

Proverbs 13:20 NIV	1 Corinthians 15:33 NAS
Ephesians 5:30 NIV	James 1:17 NIV
Philippians 2:2,3 NIV	Proverbs 17:17
Proverbs 13:20 NIV	Romans 12:15
Psalm 84:11 NIV	Proverbs 18:24
Ecclesiastes 4:9,10 NIV	Psalm 37:4,5 NIV

For Good Communication

Since I am Your child, I am a disciple of Christ—taught of the Lord and obedient to His will. Great is my peace and undisturbed composure. I am constantly renewed in the spirit of my mind [having a fresh mental and spiritual attitude] and I am putting on the new nature—the regenerate self—created in Your image, Godlike in true righteousness and holiness.

My life lovingly expresses truth [in all things speaking truly, dealing truly, living truly]. I am enfolded in love, growing up in every way and in all things into Him, Who is the Head, even Christ, the Messiah, the Anointed One. My mouth shall utter truth. I speak excellent and princely things—the opening of my lips is for right things. All the words of my mouth are righteous. There is nothing contrary to truth or crooked in me.

I incline my heart to Your testimonies, Father, and not to covetousness (robbery, sensuality, or unworthy riches). I do not love or cherish the world. The love of the Father is in me. I am set free from the lust of the flesh [craving for sensual gratification], the lust of the eyes [greedy longings of the mind], and the pride of life [assurance in my own resources or in the stability of earthly things]. I perceive and know the Truth and that nothing false is of the Truth.

I prize Your wisdom, Father, and exalt it, and it will exalt and promote me. I attend to Your Word, consent and submit to Your sayings. I keep them in the center of my heart. For they are life to me and medicine to all my flesh. I keep my heart with all diligence, for out of it flow the springs of life.

I will do nothing from factional motives [through contentiousness, strife, selfishness, or for unworthy ends] or prompted by conceit and empty arrogance. Instead, in the true spirit of humility, I regard others as better than myself. I esteem and look upon and am concerned not [merely] for my own interests, but also for the interests of others.

I let this same attitude and purpose and [humble] mind be in me that was in Christ Jesus. Thank You, Father, in Jesus' name, amen.

Scripture References

Isaiah 54:13 AMP

Romans 12:2 AMP

Ephesians 4:23,24 AMP

Ephesians 4:15 AMP

Proverbs 8:6,8 AMP

Psalm 119:36 AMP

1 John 2:15,16,21 AMP

Proverbs 4:8,20-23 AMP

Philippians 2:2-5 AMP

For Confidence in Your Relationships

Father, I thank You for the ever-developing intimate relationship I have with You. For You have been my hope, O Sovereign Lord, my confidence since my youth. From birth I have relied on You; You brought me forth from my mother's womb. I will ever praise You.

You alone are the Source of my confidence, faith, hope, love, peace, and forgiveness. Also, I thank You for my family, church family, and friends who are here to help me develop emotionally, relationally, and spiritually. I am a friend to all who fear You, to all who follow Your precepts.

Spiritually alive, we have access to everything Your Spirit is doing, and we can't be judged by unspiritual critics. Isaiah's question, "Is there anyone around who knows God's Spirit, anyone who knows what He is doing?" has been answered: Christ knows, and we have Christ's Spirit.

Your Word communicates ideas, gives me under-standing about who I am and who I am not. It is alive, dividing asunder my spirit and soul, discerning what is within me, exposing the unhealed emotional wounds and unmet needs. I submit to You, my Lord and my God, and allow Your Word to shape my life so that I may identify and settle the unresolved issues that have driven me to form unhealthy relationships in the past. I forget those things that are behind me and reach forth unto those things that are before me.

Jesus, I thank You for meeting my every need, and because I am complete in You, I don't look to another human being to bring me fulfillment. I resist the temptation to take responsibility for the behavior of others, and I assume responsibility for my own actions. You have made me glad, and I do not look to others to make me happy.

Lord, You are my confidence, and You will keep my foot from being snared. You will never leave me without support. I am confident in my relationships because You are my Lord and Master; I am a partaker of Your divine nature. You have given me all things that pertain unto life and godliness. I am a friend who loves at all times, and I will be there as a brother/sister to others in times of adversity.

In my relationships I encourage appropriate love, and my friends and I help one another out, not avoiding worshiping together as some do. We admit our faults to one another and pray for each other so that we may be healed. The earnest prayer of a righteous man has great power and wonderful results.

My relationships are founded on love from a pure heart, a good conscience, and a sincere faith in the name of Jesus. Amen.

Scripture References

Psalm 71:5,6 NIV

Psalm 119:63 NIV

1 Corinthians 2:15,16 MESSAGE

Hebrews 4:12

Philippians 3:13

Colossians 2:10

Psalm 92:4 NIV

Proverbs 3:26 NIV

Hebrews 13:5 AMP

2 Peter 1:3,4

Proverbs 17:17

Hebrews 10:24,25

James 5:16 TLB

1 Timothy 1:5 NIV

Maintaining Good Relations

Father, in the name of Jesus, I will not withhold good from those to whom it is due [its rightful owners] when it is in the power of my hand to do it. I will render to all men their dues. I will [pay] taxes to whom taxes are due, revenue to whom revenue is due, respect to whom respect is due, and honor to whom honor is due.

I will not lose heart and grow weary and faint in acting nobly and doing nobly and right, for in due season I shall reap if I do not loosen and relax my courage and faint. So then, as occasion and opportunity open up to me, I will do good [morally] to all people [not only being useful or profitable to them, but also doing what is for their spiritual good and advantage]. I will be mindful to be a blessing, especially to those of the household of faith [those who belong to Your family with me, the believers].

I will not contend with a man for no reason—when he has done me no wrong. If possible, as far as it depends on me, I purpose to live at peace with everyone. Amen.

Scripture References

Proverbs 3:27 AMP   Proverbs 3:30 AMP

Romans 13:7 AMP   Romans 12:18 AMP

Galatians 6:9,10 AMP

When Desiring To Marry

Father, here I am at Your throne asking You for mercy and grace to help me in this struggle of being single. Your grace is sufficient to displace this feeling of desperation. By faith I pray that Your name will be hallowed in my life and that Your Kingdom come and Your will be done on earth even as it is in heaven.

By faith I decree that whether I marry or remain single, I will not live carelessly, unthinkingly. I will make sure I understand what You, my Master, wants. All my ways seem innocent to me, but I ask You to weigh my motives. If it is Your will, I will be married. But whether I marry or don't marry, I will let the peace of Christ rule in my heart and be thankful.

According to Your Word, he/she who finds a wife/husband finds what is good and receives favor from You. A wife/husband of noble character is her husband's/his wife's crown, but a disgraceful wife/husband is like decay in his/her bones.

Lord, I am not looking for anyone to rescue me from being single, because I am complete in You. I trust You to bring the right person into my life so that we may bring out the best in each other and encourage each other to be all that You created each of us to be.

I delight myself in You, and You will give me the desires of my heart. I commit my way to You and will be still before You, waiting patiently for You to make Your will known to me. I resist the temptation to become angry; fretting and worry shall be far from me, because my hope is in You, Lord.

May You, Father, the God of peace, equip me with everything good for doing Your will, and may You work in me what is pleasing to You, through Jesus Christ, to Whom be glory for ever and ever. Amen.

Scripture References

Hebrews 4:16	Proverbs 18:22 NIV
2 Corinthians 12:9	Proverbs 12:4 NIV
Matthew 6:9,10	Colossians 2:10
Ephesians 5:17 MESSAGE	Psalm 37:4,5,8,9 NIV
James 4:15	Hebrews 13:20,21 NIV
Proverbs 16:2 NIV	Colossians 3:15 NIV

Knowing God's Plan for Marriage

Unto You, O Lord, do I bring my life. O my God, I trust in, lean on, rely on, and am confident in You. Let me not be put to shame or [my hope in You] be disappointed; let not my enemies (rejection, hurt, inferiority, unworthiness) triumph over me.

Father, it is written, "For I know the thoughts and plans that I have for you, says the Lord, thoughts and plans for welfare and peace and not for evil, to give you hope in your final outcome. Then you will call upon Me, and you will come and pray to Me, and I will hear and heed you. Then you will seek Me, inquire for, and require Me [as a vital necessity] and find Me when you search for Me with all your heart. I will be found by you, says the Lord" (Jer. 29:11-14 AMP).

In the name of Jesus, I always pray and do not turn coward (faint, lose heart, and give up).

Father, I am looking for Your plan, Your answer for my life. It is my desire to be married. But I must be sure in my decision that I am living as You intend and accepting whatever situation You have put me into. According to Your Word, marriage will bring extra problems that I may not need to face at this time in my life.

All the ways of a man or woman are pure in his or her own eyes, but You, Lord, weigh the spirits (the thoughts and intents of the heart). Therefore, I roll my works upon You [commit and trust them wholly to You; You will cause my thoughts to become agreeable to Your will, and] so shall my plans be established and succeed.

Because You, Lord, are my Shepherd, I have everything I need!

You let me rest in the meadow grass and lead me beside the quiet streams. You restore my health and give me new strength. You help me do what honors You the most.

Even when walking through the dark valley of death, I will not be afraid, for You are close beside me, guarding and guiding me all the way.

You provide delicious food for me in the presence of my enemies. You have welcomed me as Your guest; my blessings overflow!

Your goodness and unfailing kindness shall be with me all of my life, and afterward I will live with You forever in Your home.

In Jesus' name I pray, amen.

Scripture References

Psalm 25:1,2 AMP

Proverbs 16:2,3 AMP

Luke 18:1 AMP

Psalm 23:1-6 TLB

1 Corinthians 7:1,2 TLB

Finding a Mate

Introduction

In our ministry we hear from many men and women who desire to be married. If that is your desire, I encourage you to ask the Lord to prepare you for marriage. Submit to God's future plans for your life, and purpose to please Him. Do not make your deliberations, without knowing His will, at the expense of your personal spiritual growth and transformation. Going from glory to glory (2 Cor. 3:18) is not dependent on having a spouse.

Most of the time, each partner brings a lot of emotional baggage into the marriage relationship. As you prepare for marriage, remember that the anointing that was upon Jesus (Luke 4:18,19) is within you. This anointing will destroy every yoke of bondage (Isa. 10:27) as God exposes emotional wounds and heals your brokenness.

Knowing the reality of your completeness in Christ Jesus will enable you to enter into a healthy relationship, one in which both you and your partner will grow together spiritually and in every other area of life. Seeking first the Kingdom of God and His righteousness (Matt. 6:33), doing those things that are pleasing in His sight (1 John 3:22), will prepare you to be the person designed by Him to fulfill the role of husband or wife.

This prayer is written for your own growth and benefit.

Prayer

Father, I come before You in the name of Jesus, asking for Your will to be done in my life as I look to You for a marriage partner. I submit to the constant ministry of transformation by the Holy Spirit, making my petition known to You.

Prepare me for marriage by bringing everything to light that has been hidden—wounded emotions, walls of denial, emotional isolation, silence or excessive talking, anger, or rigidity [*name any wall that separates you from healthy relationships and God's love and grace*]. The weapons of my warfare are not carnal, but mighty through You, Lord, to the pulling down of strongholds.

I know the One in Whom I have placed my confidence, and I am perfectly certain that the work, whether I remain unmarried or marry, is safe in Your hands until that day.

Because I love You, Lord, and because I am called according to Your plan, everything that happens to me fits into a pattern for good. In Your foreknowledge, You chose me to bear the family likeness of Your Son. You chose me long ago; when the time came You called me, You made me righteous in Your sight, and then You lifted me to the splendor of life as Your child.

I lay aside every weight, and the sins which so easily ensnare me, and run with endurance the race that is set before me, looking unto Jesus, the Author and Finisher of my faith, Who for the joy that was set before Him endured the cross, despising the shame, and has sat down at the right hand of Your throne. I consider Him Who endured such hostility from sinners against Himself, lest I become weary and discouraged in my soul. I remember that He makes intercession for me.

I turn my back on the turbulent desires of youth and give my positive attention to goodness, integrity, love, and peace in company with all those who approach You, Lord, in sincerity. I have nothing to do with silly and ill-informed controversies, which lead inevitably to strife. As Your servant, I am not a person of strife. I seek to be kind to all, ready and able to teach. I seek to be tolerant and have the ability to gently correct those who oppose Your message.

Father, I desire and earnestly seek (aim at and strive after) first of all Your Kingdom and Your righteousness (Your way of doing and being right), and then all these things taken together will be given me besides. So I do not worry and will not be anxious about tomorrow.

I am persuaded that I can trust You because You first loved me. You chose me in Christ before the foundation of the world. In Him the whole fullness of Deity (the Godhead) continues to dwell in bodily form [giving complete expression of the divine nature]; and I am in Him, made full and have come to the fullness of life [in Christ].

I am filled with the Godhead—Father, Son, and Holy Spirit—and I reach toward full spiritual stature. And He (Christ) is the Head of all rule and authority [of every angelic principality and power]. So, because of Jesus, I am complete; Jesus is my Lord.

I come before You, Father, expressing my desire for a Christian mate. I petition that Your will be done in my life. Now I enter into that blessed rest by adhering to, trusting in, and relying on You.

In Jesus' name, amen.

Scripture References

Matthew 6:10

1 Corinthians 4:5

2 Corinthians 10:4

2 Timothy 1:12 PHILLIPS

Romans 8:28-30 PHILLIPS

Hebrews 12:1-3 NKJV

Romans 8:34

2 Timothy 2:22-25 PHILLIPS

Matthew 6:33,34 AMP

1 John 4:19

Ephesians 1:4

Colossians 2:9,10 AMP, NKJV

Matthew 6:10

Hebrews 4:10

John 14:1 AMP

For Your Future Spouse

Father, I seek first Your Kingdom and Your righteousness, and all things shall be mine as well. I know that You love me and that I can trust Your Word as expressed in Your Son, Jesus Christ: For in Him the whole fullness of Deity (the Godhead) continues to dwell in bodily form [giving complete expression of the divine nature]. And I am in Him, made full and have come to the fullness of life [in Christ I, too, am filled with the Godhead—Father, Son, and Holy Spirit—and reach full spiritual stature]. And Christ is the Head of all rule and authority [of every angelic principality and power]. Because of Jesus, I am complete; He is my Lord.

I come before You, Father, desiring a Christian mate. I petition that Your will be done in my life, and I enter into Your blessed rest by adhering to, trusting in, and relying on You.

Father, You desire that I live a life free from care, that I should be content and satisfied in every situation that I am in, and that I should not be anxious or worried about anything. You have said that if I am willing and obedient to Your Word, You will give me the desires of my heart. It is my desire that someday I will be married to the person You have chosen for me.

I pray for him/her. Father, especially help him/her to grow in love, Your kind of love. A friend loves at all times, and I desire for my spouse to be my very best friend. I desire that my spouse be a person who shares the same love that I have for You, someone who will be one in spirit and purpose with me.

I ask You to send mature men and women into our lives to give us good, godly counsel and to teach us how we should love each other and care for our family. Teach us both what You expect husbands and wives to do and how we ought to behave toward each other. Reveal to our hearts Your Word concerning the marriage relationship and correct any wrong thinking in our lives. Grant us knowledge through godly people, books, tapes, and preaching that will give us understanding concerning relationships, so that we can avoid damaging the relationship You desire for us.

Father, I trust You to lead me and guide me by Your Holy Spirit so that when Your perfect time is right, I will have the wisdom, discretion, and discernment to know that my choice and Yours are the same for my life-mate. I am secure with the mind and the spirit that You have given me to make this decision.

I pray that the eyes of my future spouse's understanding will be opened so that he/she will have complete knowledge of Your will in all spiritual wisdom and understanding. I pray that he/she will live a life that is worthy of You, Lord, and pleasing to You in every way. Thank You that he/she will always be involved in doing good deeds, and have a strong, growing relationship with You. I pray that our commitment to each other will continually grow as we draw closer to You.

In Jesus' name I pray, amen.

Scripture References

Matthew 6:33 RSV	Psalm 37:4,5
Colossians 2:9,10 AMP	Proverbs 17:17
Colossians 2:10 NKJV	Philippians 2:2-7
Matthew 6:10	Ephesians 5:22-25
Hebrews 4:3,10 AMP	Psalm 130:5
Philippians 4:6,11 AMP	Genesis 2:18-24
Isaiah 1:19	Colossians 1:9,10

For Favor

Father, in the name of Jesus, You make Your face to shine upon me and enlighten me. You are gracious (kind, merciful, and giving favor) to me. I am the head and not the tail, above only and not beneath.

Thank You for Your favor for me because I seek Your Kingdom and Your righteousness and diligently seek good. I am a blessing to You, Lord, and a blessing to _____ (name them: family, neighbors, business associates, etc.). Grace (favor) is with me, because I love the Lord Jesus in sincerity. Because I am Your beloved child, You extend favor, honor, and love to me, so that I am always flowing in Your love, Father. You are pouring out upon me the spirit of favor. You crown me with glory and honor, for I am Your child—Your workmanship.

I am a success today. I am someone very special with You. I am growing in You—waxing strong in spirit. Father, You give me knowledge and skill in all learning and wisdom.

You make me to find favor, compassion, and loving-kindness with _____(names). I obtain favor in the sight of all who look upon me this day, in the name of Jesus. I am filled with Your fullness—rooted and grounded in love. You are doing exceeding abundantly above all that I ask or think, for Your mighty power is taking over in me.

Thank You, Father, that I am well-favored by You and by man, in Jesus' name! Amen.

Scripture References

Numbers 6:25 AMP

Deuteronomy 28:13

Matthew 6:33

Proverbs 11:27

Ephesians 6:24

Luke 6:38

Zechariah 12:10 AMP

Luke 2:52

Psalm 8:5

Ephesians 2:10

Luke 2:40

Daniel 1:17

Daniel 1:9 AMP

Esther 2:15

Ephesians 3:17,19,20

Part V

Prayers for Your Home

To Bless Your Home

Introduction

As the head of the family (whether you are living alone as a single person or heading a single parent family), it is your privilege and duty to pray for the household in your charge and anyone under your care and authority.

I.

Prayer of Blessing for the Household

Father, as the priest and head of this household, I declare and decree, "As for me and my house, we will serve the Lord" (Josh. 24:15).

Praise be to You, the God and Father of our Lord Jesus Christ, for You have blessed us in the heavenly realms with every spiritual blessing in Christ. We reverence You and worship You in spirit and in truth.

Lord, we acknowledge and welcome the presence of Your Holy Spirit here in our home. We thank You, Father, that Your Son, Jesus, is here with us because we are gathered together in His name.

Lord God, Your divine power has given us everything we need for life and godliness through our knowledge of You Who called us by Your own glory and goodness.

As spiritual leader of this home, I declare on the authority of Your Word that my family will be mighty in the land; this generation of the upright will be blessed.

Father, You delight in the prosperity of Your people; and we thank You that wealth and riches are in our house and that our righteousness endures forever.

In the name of Jesus, amen.

Scripture References

Revelation 1:6	2 Peter 1:3 NIV
Joshua 24:15	Psalm 112:2 NIV
Ephesians 1:3 NIV	Psalm 35:27 NAS
John 4:23	Psalm 112:3
Matthew 18:20	

II.

Prayer of Blessing at the Table

Introduction

This prayer was written for the head of the household to pray not only to thank and praise God for His blessings, but also to cleanse and consecrate the food received and to sanctify the family members who partake of it.

Prayer

Father, thank You for giving to us our daily bread. We receive this food with thanksgiving and praise. You bless our bread and our water, and You take sickness out of the midst of us.

In the name of Jesus, we call this food clean, wholesome, and pure nourishment to our bodies. Should there
be any deadly thing herein, it shall not harm us, for the
Spirit of life in Christ Jesus makes us free from the law of
sin and death.

In the name of Jesus, amen.

Scripture References

Matthew 6:11	Mark 16:18
1 Timothy 4:4 NIV	Romans 8:2
Exodus 23:25	

III.

Prayer of Blessing for Children

Introduction

In his book *Jewish Customs and Ceremonies,* Ben Edidin
wrote, "The [Hebrew] father's place in the [traditional
Jewish] home is fittingly shown by the beautiful custom of
blessing the children, a custom which dates back to Isaac
and Jacob. To this day, in many homes, the father blesses
his children on Friday nights, on Rosh Hashanah eve and
on Yom Kippur before leaving for the synagogue....

"In very ancient times, the father or patriarch was the
ruler of home and family. He made laws and enforced them.

Later, however, laws were instituted by teachers, parents, judges, and kings. The father, as the master of the house, was looked up to for support and depended on for guidance."[6]

The following prayer, based on a translation of the traditional Hebrew father's blessing upon his children, may be used by the single male or female head of the household.

Prayer

Father, I receive, welcome, and acknowledge each of my children as a delightful blessing from You. I speak Your blessings upon them and over them.

Children, I bless you in the name of Jesus, proclaiming the blessings of God, my Redeemer, upon you. May He give you wisdom, a reverential fear of God, and a heart of love.

May He create in you the desire to attend to His words, a willing and obedient heart that you may consent and submit to His sayings and walk in His ways. May your eyes look straight ahead with purpose for the future. May your tongue be as the pen of a ready writer, writing mercy and kindness upon the tablets of your heart. May you speak the truth in love. May your hands do the works of the Father; may your feet walk the paths that He has foreordained for you.

---

[6] Ben M. Edidin, *Jewish Customs and Ceremonies* (New York, NY: Hebrew Publishing Company, 1941), p. 23.

I have no greater joy than this: to hear that my children are living their lives in the truth.

May the Lord prepare you and your future mate to love and honor one another, and may He grant to your union upright sons and daughters who will live in accordance with His Word. May your source of livelihood be honorable and secure, so that you will earn a living with your own hands. May you always worship God in spirit and in truth.

I pray above all things that you may always prosper and be in health, even as your soul prospers. "I know the thoughts and plans that I have for you, says the Lord, thoughts and plans for welfare and peace and not for evil, to give you hope in your final outcome" (Jer. 29:11 AMP).

In the name of Jesus, amen.

Scripture References

Psalm 127:3 AMP	Ephesians 4:15
Philippians 2:13 AMP	Ephesians 2:10 AMP
Proverbs 4:20	3 John 4 AMP
Isaiah 1:19 NIV	1 Thessalonians 4:11,12 NIV
Psalm 45:1	John 4:23
Proverbs 3:3 AMP	3 John 2

For Peace

Father, I thank You that You have blessed me with all spiritual blessings in Christ Jesus.

Through skillful and godly wisdom is my house (my life, my home, my family) built, and by understanding it is established [on a sound and good foundation]. And by knowledge shall its chambers [of every area] be filled with all precious and pleasant riches—great priceless treasure. The house of the [uncompromisingly] righteous shall stand. Prosperity and welfare are in my house, in the name of Jesus.

My house is securely built. It is founded on a rock—revelation knowledge of Your Word, Father. Jesus is my Cornerstone. Jesus is Lord of my household. Jesus is our Lord—spirit, soul, and body.

Whatever may be our task, we work at it heartily as [something] done for You, Lord, and not for men. We love each other with the God-kind of love, and we dwell in peace. My home is [deposited into Your charge, entrusted to Your protection and care].

Father, as for me and my house, we will serve the Lord, in Jesus' name. Hallelujah! Amen.

Scripture References

Ephesians 1:3

Proverbs 24:3,4 AMP

Proverbs 15:6 AMP

Proverbs 12:7 AMP

Psalm 112:3 AMP

Luke 6:48 AMP

Acts 4:11 AMP

Acts 16:31 AMP

Philippians 2:10,11 AMP

Colossians 3:23 AMP

Colossians 3:14,15 AMP

Acts 20:32 AMP

Joshua 24:15 AMP

For Health and Healing in Your Home

Father, in the name of Jesus, I come before You asking You to heal me. It is written that the prayer of faith will save the sick, and the Lord will raise him up. And if I have committed sins, I will be forgiven. I let go of all unforgiveness, resentment, anger, and bad feelings toward anyone.

My body is the temple of the Holy Spirit, and I desire to be in good health. I seek the truth that will make me free—both spiritually and naturally *(good eating habits, medications if necessary, and appropriate rest and exercise).* You bought me with a price, and I desire to glorify You in my body and my spirit—they both belong to You.

Thank You, Father, for sending Your Word to heal me and deliver me from all my destructions. Jesus, You are the Word Who became flesh and dwelt among us. You bore my griefs (pains) and carried my sorrows (sickness). You were pierced through for my transgressions and crushed for my iniquities, the chastening for my well-being fell upon You, and by Your scourging I am healed.

Father, I give attention to Your words and incline my ear to Your sayings. I will not let them depart from my sight, but I will keep them in the midst of my heart, for they are life and health to my whole body.

Father, You pardon all my iniquities; You heal all my diseases; You redeem my life from the pit; You crown me with loving-kindness and compassion; You satisfy my years with good things so that my youth is renewed like the eagle's.

Since the Spirit of Him Who raised Jesus from the dead dwells in me, He Who raised Christ from the dead will also give life to my mortal body through His Spirit Who dwells in me.

Thank You that I will prosper and be in health, even as my soul prospers. Amen.

Scripture References

James 5:15 NKJV	Isaiah 53:4,5 NAS
1 Corinthians 6:19,20	Proverbs 4:20-22 NAS
John 8:32	Psalm 103:3-5 NAS
Psalm 107:20	Romans 8:11 NKJV
John 1:14	3 John 2

For Safety

Father, in the name of Jesus, I lift myself up to You and pray a hedge of protection around me. I thank You, Father, that You are a wall of fire round about me and that Your angels camp around about me.

I thank You, Father, that I dwell in the secret place of the Most High and remain stable and fixed under the shadow of the Almighty. I will say of You, Lord, You are my Refuge and my Fortress, on You I lean and rely and in You I [confidently] trust! You cover me with Your pinions [feathers], and under Your wings shall I trust and find refuge. I shall not be afraid of the terror of the night, nor the arrow (the evil plots and slanders of the wicked) that flies by day. Only with my eyes will I behold and see the reward of the wicked.

Because I have made You, Lord, my Refuge, no evil shall befall me—no accident will overtake me—nor shall any plague or calamity come near me. For You will give Your angels [especial] charge over me, to accompany and defend and preserve me in all my ways [of obedience and service].

Father, because I have set my love upon You, therefore will You deliver me. I will call upon You, and You will answer me. You will be with me in trouble, and You will satisfy me with long life and will show me Your salvation. Not a hair of my head shall perish.

Thank You, Lord, for Your watch, care, and protection. In Jesus' name, amen.

Scripture References

Job 1:10

Zechariah 2:5

Psalm 34:7

Psalm 91:1,2 AMP

Psalm 91:4,5 AMP

Psalm 91:8

Psalm 91:9-11 AMP

Psalm 91:14-16 AMP

Luke 21:18

Pleading the Blood of Jesus

I.

Morning Prayer[1]

Father, I come in the name of Jesus to plead His blood on my life and on all that belongs to me, and on all over which You have made me a steward.

I plead the blood of Jesus on the portals of my mind, my body (the temple of the Holy Spirit), my emotions, and my will. I believe that I am protected by the blood of the Lamb which gives me access to the Holy of Holies.

I plead the blood on my children, on my grandchildren and their children, and on all those whom You have given me in this life.

Lord, You have said that the life of the flesh is in the blood. Thank You for this blood that has cleansed me from sin and sealed the New Covenant of which I am a partaker.

In Jesus' name, amen.

---

[1] Based on a prayer written by Joyce Meyer in *The Word, the Name and the Blood* (Tulsa: Harrison House, 1995), p. 116.

Scripture References

Exodus 12:7,13

Leviticus 17:11

1 Corinthians 6:19

1 John 1:7

Hebrews 9:6-14 AMP

Hebrews 13:20 AMP

II.

Evening Prayer [2]

Father, as I lie down to sleep, I plead the blood of Jesus upon my life—within me, around me, and between me and all evil and the author of evil.

In Jesus' name, amen.

Scripture References

Revelation 12:11

---

[2] Based on a prayer written by Mrs. C. Nuzum as recorded by Billye Brim in *The Blood and the Glory* (Tulsa: Harrison House, 1995), p. 17.

To Move to a New Location

Father, Your Word says that You will perfect that which concerns us. Your mercy and loving-kindness, O Lord, endure forever—forsake not the works of Your own hands. We bring to You our apprehensions concerning our relocation. We ask You to go before us [to make the crooked places straight] in finding a new home.

Give us wisdom to make wise decisions in choosing the movers and packers best suited to handle our possessions. We have favor, good understanding, and high esteem in the sight of You and man—with the utility companies, with the school systems, and with the banks—with everyone involved in this move.

Father, we thank You for supplying and preparing the new friends You want us to have. We are trusting You to direct us to a church where we can fellowship with like believers, in one accord, and where we are free to worship and praise You and sing to You a new song.

Father, in the name of Jesus, we commit this move to You, knowing that You provide for Your children. We trust You and delight ourselves in You, and You will give us the desires of our hearts.

We make all these requests known unto You with thanksgiving, and the peace that passes all understanding shall guard our hearts and minds. You will keep us in perfect peace because our minds are stayed on You.

We trust in You, Father, with all of our hearts. We lean not unto our own understanding; but in all of our ways we thank You, Father, for Your blessing on this move.

In the name of Jesus, amen.

Scripture References

Psalm 138:8 AMP

Isaiah 45:2 AMP

James 1:5

Proverbs 3:4 AMP

Hebrews 10:25 AMP

Acts 2:1,46 AMP

Acts 4:34

Philippians 2:2

Isaiah 42:10 AMP

Psalm 40:3 AMP

Psalm 96:1 AMP

Psalm 98:1 AMP

Psalm 149:1 AMP

Psalm 37:4,5 AMP

Philippians 4:6,7

Isaiah 26:3 AMP

Proverbs 3:5,6

Part VI

Prayers for
Lifestyle Success

To Get Past the Past

Father, I realize my helplessness in saving myself, and I glory in what Christ Jesus has done for me. I let go—put aside all past sources of my confidence—counting them worth less than nothing, in order that I may experience Christ and become one with Him.

Lord, I have received Your Son, and He has given me the authority (power, privilege, and right) to become Your child.

I [unfold my past] and put into proper perspective those things that are behind. I have been crucified with Christ, and I no longer live, but Christ lives in me. The life I live in the body, I live by faith in the Son of God, Who loved me and gave Himself for me. I trust in You, Lord, with all my heart and lean not on my own understanding. In all my ways I acknowledge You, and You will make my paths straight.

I want to know Christ and the power of His resurrection and the fellowship of sharing in His sufferings, becoming like Him in His death, and so, somehow, to attain to the resurrection from the dead. So, whatever it takes, I will be one who lives in the fresh newness of life of those who are alive from the dead.

I don't mean to say that I am perfect. I haven't learned all I should yet, but I keep working toward that day when I will finally be all that Christ saved me for and wants me to be.

I am bringing all my energies to bear on this one thing: Regardless of my past, I look forward to what lies ahead. I strain to reach the end of the race and receive the prize for which You are calling me up to heaven because of what Christ Jesus did for me.

In His name I pray, amen.

Scripture References

Philippians 3:7-9 TLB

Proverbs 3:5,6 NIV

John 1:12 AMP

Philippians 3:10,11 NIV

Psalm 32:5 AMP

Romans 6:4

Philippians 3:13

Philippians 3:12-14 TLB

Galatians 2:20 NIV

For Emotional Healing

Father, in the name of Jesus, I come to You with a feeling of shame and emotional hurt. I confess my transgressions to You [continually unfolding the past till all is told]. You are faithful and just to forgive me and to cleanse me of all unrighteousness. You are my Hiding Place, and You, Lord, preserve me from trouble. You surround me with songs and shouts of deliverance. I have chosen life. According to Your Word, You saw me while I was being formed in my mother's womb; and on the authority of Your Word, I was wonderfully made. Now I am Your handiwork, recreated in Christ Jesus.

Father, You have delivered me from the spirit of fear, and I shall not be ashamed. Neither shall I be confounded and depressed. You gave me beauty for ashes, the oil of joy for mourning, and the garment of praise for the spirit of heaviness that I might be called a tree of righteousness, the planting of the Lord, that You might be glorified. I speak out in psalms, hymns, and spiritual songs, offering praise with my voice and making melody with all my heart to You. Just as David did in 1 Samuel 30:6, I encourage myself in You.

I believe in You, Lord, Who raised Jesus from the dead. He was betrayed and put to death because of my misdeeds and was raised to secure my (acquittal), [absolving me from all guilt before You]. Father, You anointed Jesus and sent Him to bind up and heal my broken heart and liberate me from the shame of my youth and the imperfections of my caretakers. In His name, I choose to forgive all those who have wronged me in any way. You will not leave me without support as I complete the forgiveness process. I take comfort and am encouraged and confidently say, "The Lord is my Helper; I will not be seized with alarm...What can man do to me?" (Heb. 13:6 AMP).

My spirit is Your candle, Lord, searching all the inmost parts of my being, and the Holy Spirit leads me into all truth. When reality exposes shame and emotional pain, I remember that the sufferings of this present life are not worth being compared with the glory that is about to be revealed to me and in me and for me and conferred on me! The chastisement [needful to obtain] my peace and well-being was upon Jesus, and with the stripes [that wounded] Him, I was healed and made whole. As Your child, Father, I have a joyful and confident hope of eternal salvation. This hope will never disappoint, delude, or shame me, for Your love has been poured out in my heart through the Holy Spirit Who has been given to me.

In Jesus' name I pray, amen.

Scripture References

Psalm 32:5-7 AMP

1 John 1:9

Deuteronomy 30:19

Psalm 139:13-16 AMP

Ephesians 2:10 AMP

2 Timothy 1:7

Isaiah 54:4 AMP

Isaiah 61:3

Ephesians 5:19 AMP

Romans 4:24,25 AMP

Isaiah 61:1 AMP

Mark 11:25

Hebrews 13:5,6 AMP

Proverbs 20:27

John 16:13

Romans 8:18 AMP

Isaiah 53:5 AMP

Romans 5:3-5 AMP

To Overcome the Feeling of Rejection

Introduction

Rejection seems to create an identity crisis. Rejection by those in the Body of Christ is especially cruel. It happens more often than it should. When you are thrown into an identity crisis, you have the opportunity to erase old tapes that have played in your mind for a long time and replace those self-destructive thoughts with God-thoughts.

Your heavenly Father saw you and approved of you even while you were in your mother's womb (Ps. 139:13-16). He gave you survival tools that would bring you to the place where you are today. He is a loving Father Who has been waiting for you to come home to truth—the truth that will set you free (John 8:32).

Future rejection may hurt, but it will be only for a season (1 Pet. 1:6). The Word of God is your shield against all the fiery darts of the devil (Eph. 6:16,17).

For victory over your feeling of rejection, pray the following prayer in faith and joy.*

Prayer

Lord, Your Son, Jesus, is my High Priest. He understands and sympathizes with my weaknesses and this

---

* For further support, I encourage you to read Psalm 27 and the book of Ephesians in their entirety.

excruciating pain of rejection. In His name I approach Your throne of grace with confidence, so that I may receive mercy and find grace to help me in my time of need. I ask You to forgive my sins, and I receive Your mercy; I expect Your healing grace to dispel the rejection I am suffering because of the false accusations and demeaning actions of another.

Father, Jesus was despised and rejected—a Man of Sorrows, acquainted with bitterest grief. The grief of _____ turning against me and treating me as an outcast is consuming me, just as my rejection consumed Your Son, Who freely gave His life for me.

Forgive me for turning my back on Jesus and looking the other way—He was despised, and I didn't care. Yet it was my grief He bore, my sorrows that weighed Him down. He was wounded and bruised for my sins. He was beaten that I might have peace; He was lashed, and with His stripes I was healed.

In the face of rejection I will declare, "The Lord is my Light and my Salvation—whom shall I fear or dread? The Lord is the Refuge and Stronghold of my life—of whom shall I be afraid?" (Ps. 27:1 AMP).

I know right from wrong and cherish Your laws in my heart; I won't be afraid of people's scorn or their slanderous talk. Slanderous talk is temporal and fades away. Your Word will never pass away.

Father, I choose to look at the things that are eternal: Your justice and mercy shall last forever, and Your salvation from generation to generation. Your eyes are upon me, for I have right standing with You, and Your ears are attentive to my prayer. You spoke to me and asked, "Now who is going to hurt you if you are a zealous follower of that which is good?" (1 Pet. 3:13 AMP).

In my heart I set Christ apart as holy [and acknowledge Him] as Lord. I am always ready to give a logical defense to anyone who asks me to account for the hope that is in me, but I do it courteously and respectfully. I purpose [to see to it that] my conscience is entirely clear (unimpaired), so that, when I am falsely accused as an evildoer, those who threaten me abusively and revile my right behavior in Christ may come to be ashamed [of slandering my good life].

I am truly glad! There is wonderful joy ahead, even though the going is rough for a while down here. These trials are only to test my faith, to see whether or not it is strong and pure. It is being tested as fire tests gold and purifies it—and my faith is far more precious to You, Lord, than mere gold; so if my faith remains strong after being tried in the test tube of fiery trials, it will bring me much praise and glory and honor on the day of Jesus' return.

In spite of the rejection I have experienced, I declare that everything You say about me in Your Word is true:

I am blessed with all spiritual blessings in heavenly places in Christ (Eph. 1:3).

I am chosen by You, my Father (Eph. 1:4).

I am holy and without blame (Eph. 1:4).

I am Your child according to the good pleasure of Your will (Eph. 1:5).

I am accepted in the Beloved (Eph. 1:6).

I am redeemed through the blood of Jesus (Eph. 1:7).

I am a person of wisdom and prudence (Eph. 1:8).

I am an heir (Eph. 1:11).

I have a spirit of wisdom and revelation in the knowledge of Christ (Eph. 1:17).

I am saved by Your grace (Eph. 2:5).

I am seated in heavenly places in Christ Jesus (Eph. 2:6).

I am Your workmanship (Eph. 2:10).

I am near to You by the blood of Christ (Eph. 2:13).

I am a new creation (Eph. 2:15).

I am of Your household (Eph. 2:19).

I am a citizen of heaven (Eph. 2:19).

I am a partaker of Your promises in Christ (2 Pet. 1:4).

I am strengthened with might by Your Spirit (Eph. 3:16).

I allow Christ to dwell in my heart by faith (Eph. 3:17).

I am rooted and grounded in love (Eph. 3:17).

I speak the truth in love (Eph. 4:15).

I am renewed in the spirit of my mind (Eph. 4:23).

I am Your follower (Eph. 5:1).

I walk in love (Eph. 5:2).

I am light in You (Eph. 5:8).

I walk circumspectly (Eph. 5:15).

I am filled with the Spirit (Eph. 5:18).

I am more than a conqueror (Rom. 8:37).

I am an overcomer (Rev. 12:11).

I am Your righteousness in Christ Jesus (1 Cor. 1:30).

I am healed (1 Pet. 2:24).

I am free (John 8:36).

I am salt (Matt. 5:13).

I am consecrated (1 Cor. 6:11 AMP).

I am sanctified (1 Cor. 6:11).

I am victorious (1 John 5:4).

Everything You say about me is true, Lord.

In Your name I pray, amen.

Scripture References

Hebrews 4:14-16 NIV

1 John 1:9

Isaiah 53:3-5 TLB

2 Corinthians 4:18

Isaiah 51:7,8 TLB

Matthew 24:35

Psalm 119:89

1 Peter 3:12-17 AMP

1 Peter 1:6,7 TLB

To Let Go of Bitterness

Introduction

In interviews with divorced men and women, I have been encouraged to write a prayer on overcoming bitterness.

Often the injustice of the situation in which these people find themselves creates deep hurts, wounds in the spirit, and anger that is so near the surface that the individuals involved risk sinking into the abyss of bitterness and revenge. Their thoughts may turn inward as they consider the unfairness of the situation and dwell on how badly they have been treated.

In a family divorce situation, bitterness sometimes distorts ideas of what is best for the child/children involved. One parent (and sometimes both parents) will use the child/children against the other.

Unresolved anger often moves one marriage partner to hurt the one he or she holds responsible for the hurt and sense of betrayal that is felt.

There is healing available. There is a way of escape for all who will turn to the Healer, obeying Him and trusting Him.

Prayer

Father, life seems so unjust, so unfair. The pain of rejection is almost more than I can bear. My past relationships have ended in strife, anger, rejection, and separation.

Lord, help me to let go of all bitterness and indignation and wrath (passion, rage, bad temper) and resentment (anger and animosity).

You are the One Who binds up and heals the broken-hearted. I receive Your anointing that destroys every yoke of bondage. I receive emotional healing by faith, and I thank You for giving me the grace to stand firm until the process is complete.

Thank You for wise counselors. I acknowledge the Holy Spirit as my wonderful Counselor. Thank You for helping me work out my salvation with fear and trembling, for it is You, Father, Who works in me to will and to act according to Your good purpose.

In the name of Jesus, I choose to forgive those who have wronged me. I purpose to live a life of forgiveness because You have forgiven me. With the help of the Holy Spirit, I get rid of all bitterness, rage, anger, brawling, and slander, along with every form of malice. I desire to be kind and compassionate to others, forgiving them, just as in Christ You forgave me.

With the help of the Holy Spirit, I make every effort to live in peace with all men and to be holy, for I know that without holiness no one will see You, Lord. I purpose to see to it that I do not miss Your grace and that no bitter root grows up within me to cause trouble and defile me or others.

I will watch and pray that I enter not into temptation or cause others to stumble.

Thank You, Father, that You watch over Your Word to perform it and that whom the Son has set free is free indeed. I declare that I have overcome resentment and bitterness by the blood of the Lamb and by the word of my testimony.

In Jesus' name, amen.

Scripture References

Ephesians 4:31 AMP	Ephesians 4:31,32 NIV
Luke 4:18	Hebrews 12:14,15 NIV
Isaiah 10:27	Matthew 26:41
Proverbs 11:14	Romans 14:21
John 15:26 AMP	Jeremiah 1:12 AMP
Philippians 2:12,13 NIV	John 8:36
Matthew 5:44	Revelation 12:11

To Break the Curse of Abuse

Introduction

**Christ redeemed us from the curse of the law
by becoming a curse for us, for it is written:
"Cursed is everyone who is hung on a tree."**

Galatians 3:13 NIV

On a Sunday morning after I had taught a lesson
titled "Healing for the Emotionally Wounded," a young
man wanted to speak with me. I listened intently as he
told me that he had just been released from jail and was
now on probation for physically abusing his family. His
wife had filed for divorce, and he was living alone. It was
not easy for him to confess his sin to me, and I was
impressed by his humble attitude.

He said, "I am glad that this message is being given
in the Church and that the abused can receive ministry.
Is there anywhere that the abuser can go to receive spiritual help?"

He shared with me that he was attending a support
group for abusers. He desired to commit to a church
where he could receive forgiveness and acceptance. He
knew that any lasting change would have to be from the
inside out by the Spirit. I prayed with him, but it would
be three years before I could write a prayer for the abuser.

As I read, studied, and sought the Lord, I discovered that the abuser is usually a person who has been abused. Often the problem is a generational curse that has been in the family of the abuser for as far back as anyone can remember. Many times the abuser declares that he will never treat his wife and children as he has been treated, but in spite of his resolve, he finds himself reacting in the same violent manner.

The generational curse can be reversed if the abuser is willing to allow God to remove the character flaws that have held him in bondage.

If you are an abuser, I encourage you to pray this prayer for yourself until it becomes a reality in your life. If you know someone who is an abuser, pray it as a prayer of intercession in the third person.

Prayer

I receive and confess that Jesus is my Lord, and I ask that Your will be done in my life.

Father, You have delivered me from the dominion of darkness and have transferred (brought) me into the Kingdom of the Son of Your love. Once I was darkness, but now I am light in You; I walk as a child of Light. The abuse is exposed and reproved by the Light—it is made visible and clear; and where everything is visible and clear, there is light.

Help me to grow in grace (undeserved favor, spiritual strength) and recognition and knowledge and understanding of my Lord and Savior, Jesus Christ, so that I may experience Your love and trust You to be a Father to me.

The history of my earthly family is filled with abusive behavior, much hatred, strife, and rage. The painful memory of past abuse *(verbal, emotional, physical, and/or sexual)* has caused me to be hostile and abusive to others.

I desire to be a doer of the Word and not a hearer only. No matter which way I turn, I can't make myself do right. I want to, but I can't. When I want to do good, I don't; and when I try not to do wrong, I do it anyway. It seems that sin still has me in its evil grasp. This pain has caused me to hurt others and myself. In my mind I want to be Your willing servant, but instead I find myself still enslaved to sin.

I confess my sin of abuse, resentment, and hostility toward others, and I ask You to forgive me. You are faithful and just to forgive my sin and cleanse me from all unrighteousness. I am tired of reliving the past in my present life, perpetuating the generational curse of anger and abuse.

Jesus was made a curse for me; therefore, Lord, I put on Your whole armor that I may be able to successfully stand against all the strategies and the tricks of the devil. I thank You that the evil power of abuse is broken, overthrown, and cast down. I submit myself to You and resist the devil. The need to hurt others no longer controls my family or me.

In Jesus' name, amen.

Scripture References

Romans 10:9   Romans 7:18-25 TLB

Matthew 6:10   1 John 1:9

Colossians 1:13 AMP   Galatians 3:13

Ephesians 5:8,13 AMP   Ephesians 6:11,12 TLB

2 Peter 3:18 AMP   2 Corinthians 10:5

James 1:22   James 4:7

To Forget Failure

Devotional Reading

May the Lord answer [me] when [I am]
    in distress;
      may the name of the God of Jacob
      protect [me].

May he send [me] help from the sanctuary
    and grant [me] support from Zion.

May he remember all [my] sacrifices
    and accept [my] burnt offerings.

May he give [me] the desire of [my] heart
    and make all [my] plans succeed.

[I] will shout for joy when [I am] victorious
    and will lift up [my banner] in the name of
    [my] God. May the Lord grant all [my] requests.

Now I know that the Lord saves his anointed;
    he answers him [her] from his holy heaven
    with the saving power of his right hand.

Some trust in chariots and some in horses,
    but [I] trust in the name of the
      Lord [my] God.

They are brought to their knees and fall,
    but [I] rise up and stand firm.

O Lord, save the king [queen]!
Answer [me] when [I] call!

Psalm 20:1-9 NIV

Meditation

The writer of Psalm 20 lived under the Old Covenant.
Today we are living in the age of a new covenant and do
not offer up sacrifices of animals. Instead, Jesus, the Lamb
of God, gave Himself to be crucified on the cross of
Calvary as the perfect sacrifice for our sins and for the sins
of the whole world (1 John 2:2). In so doing, He provided
for us everything we need in this life and the next:

The high priest carries the blood of animals
into the Most Holy Place as a sin offering, but the
bodies are burned outside the camp.

And so Jesus also suffered outside the city gate
to make the people holy through his own blood.
Let us, then, go to him outside the camp, bearing
the disgrace he bore.

For here we do not have an enduring city, but
we are looking for the city that is to come.

Through Jesus, therefore, let us continually
offer to God a sacrifice of praise—the fruit of lips
that confess his name.

And do not forget to do good and to share
with others, for with such sacrifices God is pleased.

Hebrews 13:11-16 NIV

Prayer

Father, You see my disappointment and distress over this setback. I poured many hours of study and preparation into this situation *(job, business, relationship, marriage, etc.)*. My plans were carefully laid. I believed and expected it to prosper, but now it seems that all of my work was in vain.

I look to You, O Lord. Help me to learn of You, even in the midst of this adversity, and to remain strong in You and in Your mighty power.

Father, I believe that You brought me to this point in my life, and I will not be afraid, for You turn into good anything that is intended for my undoing.

You are God, and there is no other; there is none like You. You know the end from the beginning, from ancient times, what is still to come. Your purpose in this situation will stand, and You will do all that You please.

I refuse to be amazed and bewildered at the fiery ordeal that is taking place to test my quality, as though something strange (unusual and alien to me and my position) were befalling me.

Father, I remember that Your blessing brings wealth, and You add no trouble to it. There is surely a future hope for me, and my hope will not be cut off. I have sown, that good might come to others; and I believe that I shall reap in due season, if I faint not.

O my soul, don't be discouraged. Don't be upset. Expect God to act! For I know that I shall again have plenty of reason to praise him for all that he will do. He is my help! He is my God!

Psalm 42:11 TLB

Lord, I offer up to You sacrifices of praise—the fruit of my lips, which confess Your name—and I will not forget to do good and to share with others, for with such sacrifices You are pleased.

In Jesus' name I pray, amen.

Scripture References

Ephesians 6:10 NIV   Proverbs 10:22 NIV

Genesis 50:20 TLB   Proverbs 23:18 NIV

Isaiah 46:8-10 NIV   Galatians 6:9

1 Peter 4:12 AMP   Hebrews 13:15,16 NIV

To Live Free From Fear

Father, when I am afraid, I will put my confidence in You. Yes, I will trust Your promises. And since I trust You, what can mere man do to me?

You have not given me a spirit of timidity, but of power and love and discipline (sound judgment). Therefore, I am not ashamed of the testimony of You, my Lord. I have not received a spirit of slavery leading to fear again, but I have received a spirit of adoption as a son/daughter, by which I cry out, "Abba! Father!"

Jesus, You delivered me, Who, through fear of death, had been living all my life as a slave to constant dread. I receive the gift You left me—peace of mind and heart! And the peace You give isn't fragile like the peace the world gives. I cast away troubled thoughts, and I choose not to be afraid. I believe in God; I believe also in You.

Lord, You are my Light and my Salvation; You protect me from danger—whom shall I fear? When evil men come to destroy me, they will stumble and fall! Yes, though a mighty army marches against me, my heart shall know no fear! I am confident that You will save me.

Thank You, Holy Spirit, for bringing these things to my remembrance when I am tempted to be afraid. I will trust in my God. In the name of Jesus I pray, amen.

Scripture References

Psalm 56:3-5 TLB

2 Timothy 1:7,8 NAS

Romans 8:15 NAS

Hebrews 2:15 TLB

John 14:1,26,27 TLB

Psalm 27:1-3 TLB

To Cast Your Cares on the Lord and Leave Them There

Father, my daily responsibilities and my feelings of inferiority, failure, guilt, and condemnation have overwhelmed me like a burden too heavy to bear. Hear me and answer me. My thoughts trouble me, and I am distraught.

Living as a single person is not easy, and anxiety continues to build as I see friends getting married. I am tired of feeling so alone. I know that I should seek first all Your Kingdom, but a need to be married is becoming an obsession—a burden that grows heavier—and depression is intensifying.

In the name of Jesus, I make the decision to cast my cares on You, my Lord, knowing that You will sustain me; You will never let the righteous fall. Lord Jesus, Your yoke is easy, and Your burden is light. I will learn from You Who walked this earth as a single person. You were tempted in all points even as I am; yet You were without sin. When anxiety is great within me, Your consolation brings joy to my soul.

You have strengthened me in my innermost being, and I resist the temptation to worry about my life, what I will eat or drink; or about my body, what I will wear. Life is more important than food, and the body more important than clothes. You are my heavenly Father Who knows that I need these things. Therefore I will seek first Your Kingdom and Your righteousness, confident that all these things will be given to me as well.

So I am learning to be content with who I am and will not put on airs. God, Your strong hand is on me; You will promote me at the right time. Thank You for giving me the grace to cast all my cares and anxieties on You. I purpose to live carefree before You, my Lord and my God; You are most careful with me.

In Jesus' name I pray, amen.

Scripture References

Psalm 38:4 NIV

Psalm 55:2 NIV

Psalm 55:22 NIV

Matthew 11:29,30 NIV

Hebrews 4:15 NKJV

Psalm 94:19 NIV

Ephesians 3:16 AMP

Matthew 6:25,26,32,33 NIV

1 Peter 5:6,7 MESSAGE

1 Peter 5:7 AMP

To Overcome Discouragement

Introduction

Moses returned to the Lord and said, "O Lord, why have you brought trouble upon this people? Is this why you sent me? Ever since I went to Pharaoh to speak in your name, he has brought trouble upon this people, and you have not rescued your people at all."

Exodus 5:22,23 NIV

Here in this passage, we find Moses discouraged, complaining to God.

It is important that we approach God with integrity and in an attitude of humility. But because we fear making a negative confession, we sometimes cross the line of honesty into the line of denial and delusion.

Let's be honest. God already knows what we are feeling. He can handle our anger, complaints, and disappointments. He understands us. He is aware of our human frailties (Ps. 103:14) and can be touched with the feelings of our infirmities (Heb. 4:15).

Whether your "trouble" is a business failure, abandonment, depression, a mental disorder, a chemical imbalance, oppression, a marriage problem, a child who is in a strange land of drugs and alcohol, financial disaster, or anything else, the following prayer is for you.

Sometimes when you are in the midst of discouragement, it is difficult to remember that you have ever known any Scripture. I admonish you to read this prayer aloud until you recognize the reality of God's Word in your spirit, soul, and body. Remember, God is watching over His Word to perform it (Jer. 1:12 AMP). He will perfect that which concerns you (Ps. 138:8).

Prayer

Lord, I do not understand why You have allowed this trouble to assail me. It was after I began to follow You in obedience that this trouble was manifested in my life. I have exhausted all my possibilities for changing my situation and circumstances and have found that I am powerless to change them. I believe; help me overcome my unbelief. Not all things are possible with man, but all things are possible with You. I humble myself before You, and You will lift me up.

I have a great High Priest Who has gone through the heavens: Jesus, Your Son. And I hold firmly to the faith I profess. My High Priest is able to sympathize with my weaknesses. He was tempted in every way, just as I am— yet was without sin. I then approach Your throne of grace with confidence, so that I may receive mercy and find grace to help me in my time of need.

In the face of discouragement, disappointment, and anger, I choose to believe that Your word to Moses is Your word to me. You are mighty to deliver. Because of Your mighty hand, You will drive out the forces that have set themselves up against me. You are the Lord, Yahweh, the Promise-Keeper, the Almighty One. You appeared to Abraham, to Isaac, and to Jacob and established Your covenant with them.

Father, I believe that You have heard my groaning, my cries. I will live to see Your promises of deliverance fulfilled in my life. You have not forgotten one word of Your promise; You are a Covenant-Keeper.

It is You Who will bring me out from under the yoke of bondage and free me from being a slave to _____. You have redeemed me with an outstretched arm and with mighty acts of judgment. You have taken me as Your own, and You are my God. You are a father to me. You have delivered me from the past that has held me in bondage and translated me into the Kingdom of love, peace, joy, and righteousness. I will no longer settle for the pain of the past. Where sin abounds, grace does much more abound.

Father, what You have promised, I will go and possess, in the name of Jesus. I am willing to take the chance, to take the risk, to get back into the good fight of faith. It is with patient endurance and steady and active persistence that I run the race, the appointed course that is set before me. I rebuke the spirit of fear, for I am established in righteousness. Oppression and destruction shall not come near me. Behold, they may gather together and stir up strife, but it is not from You, Father. Whoever stirs up strife against me shall fall and surrender to me. I am more than a conqueror through Him Who loves me.

In His name I pray, amen.

Scripture References

(This prayer is based on Exodus 5:22-6:11 and includes other verses where applicable.)

Mark 9:24 NIV	Deuteronomy 26:8
Luke 18:27	Colossians 1:13
1 Peter 5:6 NIV	Romans 5:20
Hebrews 4:14-16 NIV	1 Timothy 6:12
Exodus 6:3,4,5 AMP	Hebrews 12:1 AMP
Genesis 49:22-26 AMP	Isaiah 54:14-16 AMP
1 Kings 8:56	Romans 8:37

When Facing Sexual Temptation

And lead us not into temptation, but deliver us from evil: For thine is the kingdom, and the power, and the glory, for ever. Amen.

Matthew 6:13

Watch and pray, that ye enter not into temptation: the spirit indeed is willing, but the flesh is weak.

Matthew 26:41

The Lord knoweth how to deliver the godly out of temptations, and to reserve the unjust unto the day of judgment to be punished.

2 Peter 2:9

But thou, O Lord, art a shield for me; my glory, and the lifter up of mine head.

Psalm 3:3

Be pleased, O Lord, to deliver me: O Lord, make haste to help me.

Let them be ashamed and confounded together that seek after my soul to destroy it; let them be driven backward and put to shame that wish me evil.

Psalm 40:13,14

Thy word have I hid in mine heart, that I might not sin against thee.

Psalm 119:11

For the Lord shall be thy confidence, and shall keep thy foot from being taken.

Proverbs 3:26

In the fear of the Lord is strong confidence: and his children shall have a place of refuge.

Proverbs 14:26

Let thine eyes look right on, and let thine eyelids look straight before thee.

Turn not to the right hand nor to the left: remove thy foot from evil.

Proverbs 4:25,27

The way of the Lord is strength to the upright: but destruction shall be to the workers of iniquity.

Proverbs 10:29

He that covereth his sins shall not prosper: but whoso confesseth and forsaketh them shall have mercy.

Proverbs 28:13

Fear thou not; for I am with thee: be not dismayed; for I am thy God: I will strengthen thee; yea, I will help thee; yea, I will uphold thee with the right hand of my righteousness.

Isaiah 41:10

To Display Integrity

Father, when You test my heart, may You be pleased with my honesty. In everything I do, may I set an example by doing what is good.

In my workplace may I show integrity, seriousness, and soundness of speech that cannot be condemned, so that those who oppose me may be ashamed because they have nothing bad to say about me. I purpose to conduct myself, as David did, with integrity of heart, and with skillful hands before the people who observe me.

Father, I thank You that the integrity of the upright guides me. May I be blameless in Your sight so that I will receive a good inheritance. Let it be said of me by all men, "We know you are a person of integrity and that you teach the way of God in accordance with the truth" (Matt. 22:16 NIV).

Judge me, O Lord, according to my righteousness, according to my integrity, O Most High, and make me secure and guard me in Your righteousness. In my integrity uphold me and set me in Your presence forever.

In Jesus' name I pray, amen.

Scripture References

1 Chronicles 29:17 NIV

Titus 2:7,8 NIV

Psalm 78:72 NIV

Proverbs 11:3 NIV

Proverbs 28:10 NIV

Matthew 22:16 NIV

Psalm 7:8 NIV

Proverbs 13:6 NIV

Psalm 41:12 NIV

To Be Well-Balanced

Father, in the name of Jesus, I come boldly to Your throne of grace to receive mercy and find grace to help in time of need.

Forgive me for getting caught up in my own pride. Sometimes I behave as though I am indispensable at home, at the office, at church, and in other situations. I become irritable and fatigued, feeling that no one appreciates all that I do. Help me to step back and take a personal inventory. My spirit is Your candle, searching out all the inward parts of my being.

Jesus said, **"Come to me, all of you who are weary and over-burdened, and I will give you rest! Put on my yoke and learn from me. For I am gentle and humble in heart and you will find rest for your souls. For my yoke is easy and my burden is light"** (Matt. 11:28-30 PHILLIPS).

Lord, not only am I yoked up with You, but also with my colleagues, and others whom You have sent into my life. I am not alone, and I cannot carry these associations alone. Help me to resist the temptation to be unequally yoked together with unbelievers for the sake of financial profit.

There is a time for everything, and a season for every activity under heaven. Help me to keep my priorities in order. Help me to fulfill my call and responsibilities at home as a single person and/or single parent. While I am at work, help me to stay focused. Also, help me to take time to find rest (relief and ease and refreshment and recreation and blessed quiet) for my soul.

I cast the whole of my care [all my anxieties, all my worries, all my concerns, once and for all] on You, for You care for me affectionately and care about me watchfully. I affirm that I am well-balanced (temperate, sober of mind), vigilant, and cautious at all times; for that enemy of mine, the devil, roams around like a lion roaring [in fierce hunger], seeking someone to seize upon and devour. In the name of Jesus, I withstand him; firm in faith [against his onset— rooted, established, strong, immovable, and determined]. And after I have suffered a little while, You, the God of all grace [Who imparts all blessing and favor], Who has called me to His [own] eternal glory in Christ Jesus, will Yourself complete and make me what I ought to be, establish and ground me securely, and strengthen and settle me.

To You be the dominion (power, authority, rule) for ever and ever. Amen (so be it).

Scripture References

Hebrews 4:16 AMP	Ecclesiastes 3:1 NIV
Proverbs 20:27	Matthew 11:29 AMP
2 Corinthians 6:14	1 Peter 5:7-11 AMP

To Set Proper Priorities

Father, too often I allow urgency to dictate my schedule, and I am asking You to help me establish priorities in my work. I confess my weakness* of procrastination and lack of organization. My desire is to live purposefully and worthily and accurately as a wise (sensible, intelligent) person.

You have given me a seven-day week—six days to work and the seventh day to rest. I desire to make the most of the time [buying up each opportunity]. Help me plan my day and stay focused on my assignments.

In the name of Jesus, I demolish and smash warped philosophies concerning time management, tear down barriers erected against the truth of God, and fit every loose thought, emotion, and impulse into the structure of life shaped by Christ. I clear my mind of every obstruction and build a life of obedience into maturity.

Father, You are in charge of my work and my plans. I plan the way I want to live, but You alone make me able to live it. Help me to organize my efforts, schedule my activities, and budget my time.

Jesus, You want me to relax. It pleases You when I am not preoccupied with getting, so I can respond to God's giving. I know You, Father, and how You work. I steep my life in God-reality, God-initiative, and God-provisions.

---

* If you do not know your strengths and weaknesses, ask the Holy Spirit to reveal them to you. The Lord speaks to us: "My grace is sufficient for you, for power is perfected in weakness" (2 Cor. 12:9 NAS).

By the grace given me, I will not worry about missing out, and my everyday human concerns will be met. I purpose in my heart to seek (aim at and strive after) first of all Your Kingdom, Lord, and Your righteousness (Your way of doing and being right), and then all these things taken together will be given me besides.

Father, Your Word is my compass, and it helps me see my life as complete in Christ. I cast all my cares [anxieties, worries, and concerns] over on You, that I might be well-balanced (temperate, sober of mind), vigilant, and cautious at all times.

I tune my ears to the word of wisdom, and I set my heart on a life of understanding. I make insight my priority.

Father, You sent Jesus that I might have life and have it more abundantly. Help me remember that my relationship with You and with others is more important than anything else. Amen.

Scripture References

Ephesians 5:15,16 AMP	Matthew 6:33
Genesis 2:2 NIV	MESSAGE, AMP
2 Corinthians 10:5,6 MESSAGE	Colossians 2:10
Proverbs 16:3,9 MESSAGE	1 Peter 5:7,8 AMP
Matthew 11:29 MESSAGE, AMP	Proverbs 2:3 MESSAGE
Matthew 6:31 MESSAGE	John 10:10

A Word to the Single Parent

God has entrusted children to your care for a period of time. As someone has said, "He has given us our children on loan; they belong to Him."

You are God's representative to your child/children. To reveal the love of God to your child/children, it is imperative that you have a revelation of God's love for you. He chose you before the foundation of the world that you should be holy, even above reproach in His sight (Eph. 1:4 AMP). You cannot give that which you have not received. Believe that God is, that He is love, and that He loved you before you had done anything good or bad. He is your Father. His love is shed abroad in your heart (Rom. 5:5), and this love is developed in a tough schoolroom—the home.

Walking in love with your children is an ongoing learning process. Many times you will make mistakes, but you can learn from your mistakes. Talk with your children and confess when you have been wrong or acted contrary to love. Your heavenly Father set boundaries around you because you are His child; now you are to set boundaries for your children. Teach them to become responsible by allowing them to make choices and to suffer the consequences of their wrong decisions.

You do not want to break your child's will, but teach and train your child with understanding: "Train up a child in the way he should go: and when he is old, he will not depart from it" (Prov. 22:6).

A mother recently shared an experience while preparing to go to church on a stressful Sunday morning. Turning to her four-year-old daughter, she told her to go make up her bed. This turned into a battle of wills. The mother soon exhausted her arsenal of human weapons—threats, manipulation, and control; then she paused to pray.

Taking a deep breath she walked into her child's bedroom, only to find her dawdling. In a quiet voice she said, "Please forgive me, and forget all the threats. Here's the deal, and you are free to choose. If you make up your bed, we will go out to lunch with our friends after church as we planned. If you choose not to make your bed, you and I will come straight home from church." The child thought for a moment, then brightened up saying, "If I can choose, then I choose to make my bed."

To allow this child to choose required the mother to risk giving up something she wanted to do. She considered the cost, and was willing to pay it in order to teach her child responsibility. It requires discipline, self-control, and wisdom to set boundaries and impose reasonable consequences, because sometimes it requires the parent to suffer along with the child. This method does not work like magic, but is a day-to-day process. Every situation may not turn out as favorably as this one did.

Pray for wisdom, and be consistent with your rules for your home. Think before you react to your child. Consider your decision—is it being made to bring immediate relief and gratification to you, or to do what is best for your child? Does your decision, no matter how tough it is, issue from the love of God?

When you make a mistake, and you will sometimes, don't beat yourself up about it. If you confess it, your heavenly Father will forgive you and will cleanse you from all unrighteousness (1 John 1:9). It isn't easy to raise children without a spouse, but God is faithful. He proved Himself caring and considerate of the single parent throughout the Scriptures. He is full of grace and mercy. God is love (1 John 4:8)!

Attend a good church where you and your child can receive emotional and spiritual support. It is my prayer that the local church will recognize its responsibility for nurturing single parents and their children.

"Sons are a heritage from the Lord, children a reward from him. Like arrows in the hands of a warrior are sons born in one's youth" (Ps. 127:3,4 NIV). Thank God for this opportunity to make disciples of your children so that they may be equipped to go into all the world and make disciples to the glory of the Father.

Part VII

Prayers for
Parenting Skills

To Bring Honor to God as a Parent

Father, I come before You today bringing an offering of praise and thanksgiving so that I may honor and glorify You. Thank You for my children who are a heritage from You—they are my reward. I pray that I will order my way of life aright with my children [speaking truly, dealing truly, and living truly] for Your glory and honor.

Oh, Father, I called on You in the day of trouble, and You delivered me. I will honor and glorify You, relying on the Holy Spirit to help me teach and train my children in the nurture and admonition of the Lord.

In our home I purpose to do everything in the name of Jesus and in [dependence] upon His Person. I will work at fulfilling my responsibility to You and my children as [something done] for You and not for men. To You, Father, be all glory and honor and praise.

You are my Lord, and I desire to be a parent who honors You so that my children may see my good works and glorify You. On the authority of Your Word I affirm that I am Your purchased possession, a special person, that I should show forth Your praises. You have called me out of darkness into Your marvelous light, for which I am eternally grateful.

Grant me the wisdom that I may walk in truth, love, patience, holiness, goodness, joy, peace, and faith before my children. Your divine power has given unto me all things that pertain unto life and godliness, through the knowledge of Him Who has called me to glory and virtue.

In the name of Jesus, I submit to You because You are effectually at work in me [energizing and creating in me the power and desire] both to will and work for Your good pleasure, satisfaction, and delight in our home.

Lord, You are my God, and I purpose to progressively walk in Your ways, and to keep Your statues, commandments, and judgments. I hearken to Your voice, and the voice of a stranger I will not follow. You will make me high—in name and in honor.

Father, I will honor You by keeping Your word concerning my children. I will teach and train them in the way they are to go. In the name of Jesus, I will be a vessel unto honor, sanctified, and meet for the Master's use, and prepared unto every good work. I purpose to follow after righteousness and mercy as I rear my children tenderly in the Lord. Then I will find life, righteousness, and honor.

In the name of Jesus. Amen.

Scripture References

Psalm 50:23 AMP	2 Peter 1:3
Psalm 127:3	Philippians 2:13 AMP
Ephesians 4:15 AMP	Deuteronomy 26:16-19

Psalm 50:15   John 10:5

Ephesians 6:4   Proverbs 22:6

Colossians 3:17 AMP   2 Timothy 2:20-23

Colossians 3:23   Proverbs 21:21

1 Peter 2:9 AMP   Galatians 5:22,23,35

Parenting Skills

Father, now that I am a single parent, I ask You to be a father/mother to my child/children, and to give me strength and wisdom for the task before me. I am not sufficient of myself to think anything as of myself; but my sufficiency is of You. In every situation help me to remember that Your grace is sufficient for me; for Your strength is made perfect in weakness.

Father, my children are prone to foolishness and fads. I ask You for the grace to apply the cure that comes through tough-minded discipline. In the name of Jesus I will not provoke and exasperate my children with abusive language or harsh physical treatment, but will nurture, correct, and instruct them in the ways of righteousness. You have imparted the law of kindness to me, enabling me to resist the temptation to make unproductive threats. I will set boundaries of protection and security, training them up in the way they should go. I resist the temptation to be domineering and demanding. Instead I will show love by disciplining them, even as a shepherd tends his sheep.

Father, there is so much to do, and even when I'm tired and worn out, my children need me. I will not be [merely] concerned with my own interests, or consumed with making ends meet, but will show interest in my children's activities through participation, listening, and praise. Your words are in my heart, and I will teach them diligently to my children, and talk of them when I walk by the way, when I lie down, and when I rise up. Thank You for sending the Holy Spirit Who is my Comforter, Strengthener, and Standby.

Wisdom from above is wholehearted and straightforward, and I will remember that it is unwise to compare myself with my child or to compete with him/her. When I was a child I behaved as a child, but now that I am an adult I will to put away childish behavior, and to be an imitator of You, heavenly Father, shepherding my children with love. In the name of Jesus I pull down every controlling, manipulative attitude. I resist the temptation to coerce; instead, I will seek to lead them into paths of righteousness for Your name's sake.

In the name of Jesus, I ask You to watch over these words that I have prayed and perform them in my life. Amen.

Scripture References

Psalm 27:10	Philippians 2:4 AMP
2 Corinthians 3:5	Deuteronomy 6:7 AMP
2 Corinthians 12:9	John 14:16 AMP
Proverbs 22:15 MESSAGE	James 3:17 AMP
Ephesians 6:4 AMP	Colossians 1:13 MESSAGE
Proverbs 31:26	James 3
Proverbs 22:6	2 Corinthians 10:12
Ephesians 6:1-4	1 Corinthians 13:11 AMP
Proverbs 13:24 MESSAGE	Psalm 23:3
1 Peter 5:1-4 AMP	Jeremiah 1:12 AMP

To Parent With Wisdom

Father, I come before Your throne of grace asking for wisdom that is pure, peace-loving, considerate, submissive, full of mercy and good fruit, impartial, and sincere. You promised to give generously, without finding fault, if I ask without doubting. So, I believe that I have received, and I set my heart and mind to believe and not doubt. Give me the grace to be single-minded, stable in all I do with my children and for them.

Lord, You give wisdom, and from Your mouth come knowledge and understanding. Thank You for teaching me wisdom in the inmost place. I declare and decree that my mouth will speak words of wisdom; the utterance from my heart will give understanding. If I am wise when I instruct and correct my children, wisdom will reward me.

As an imitator of You, my heavenly Father, I will extend grace and mercy to my children. Lord, as I delight myself in You, my heart is becoming more flexible, and I am replacing rigidity with prudence and common sense.

In the name of Jesus, I repent of and renounce the berating of my children, asking for Your forgiveness for those times that I have spoken reckless words that have pierced my children like a sword. Cause my words of wisdom to bring healing to their emotional wounds. In the name of Jesus, I rebuke and renounce, crush and smash, the stronghold of pride that breeds quarrels with my children. I will seek out wise counsel and listen to sound advice. The fear of the Lord teaches me wisdom, and humility comes before honor. I will appropriately humble myself by admitting the wrongs I have done to my children, and will ask for their forgiveness so that we may all be healed.

I desire to be a wise person who is discerning, and to speak pleasant words that promote instruction. My heart will guide my mouth, and my lips will promote instruction. By wisdom our house is built, and through understanding it is established; through knowledge its rooms are filled with rare and beautiful treasures. Give me the grace to be quick to listen, slow to speak, and slow to anger. Jesus has been made unto me wisdom, and I will keep myself under control.

Father, forgive me for the times I have corrected my children in anger. It is the rod of correction[9] that imparts wisdom; my children will not have to raise themselves. I will discipline them while I still have the chance and will resist the temptation to indulge them. Thank You for hearing my prayer, in the name of Jesus. Amen.

---

[9] Thy rod and thy staff, they comfort me (Psalm 23). The rod of correction is "not just a swat…it is everything you do to shape your child." Dr. Frank Minirth, Dr. Brian Newman, and Dr. Paul Warren, *The Father Book: An Instruction Manual*, (Nashville, TN: Thomas Nelson, Inc., 1992), p. 89.

Scripture References

James 3:17 AMP

James 1:5 NIV

Proverbs 2:6

Psalm 51:6

Psalm 49:3

Proverbs 9:10-12 NIV

Proverbs 12:18

Proverbs 13:10 NIV

Proverbs 24:6 AMP

James 5:16

Proverbs 12:20 NIV

Proverbs 16:21-23 NIV

Proverbs 24:3,4 NIV

James 1:19 AMP

1 Corinthians 1:30

Proverbs 29:11

Proverbs 22:15

Proverbs 19:15 MESSAGE

Proverbs 15:33

To Know God's Will

Father, in Jesus' name, I thank You that You are instructing me in the way I should go and that You are guiding me with Your eye. I thank You for Your guidance and leading concerning Your will, Your plan, and Your purpose for my life. I do hear the voice of the Good Shepherd, for I know You and follow You. You lead me in the paths of righteousness for Your name's sake.

Thank You, Father, that my path is growing brighter and brighter until it reaches the full light of day. As I follow You, Lord, I believe my path is becoming clearer each day.

Thank You, Father, that Jesus was made unto me wisdom. Confusion is not a part of my life. I am not confused about Your will for my life. I trust in You and lean not unto my own understanding. As I acknowledge You in all of my ways, You are directing my paths. I believe that as I trust in You completely, You will show me the path of life. Amen.

Scripture References

Psalm 32:8	1 Corinthians 1:30
John 10:2-5,11,14	1 Corinthians 14:33
Psalm 23:3	Proverbs 3:5,6
Proverbs 4:18	Psalm 16:11

To Develop Patience

Father, I come before You in the name of Jesus. I desire to meditate, consider, and inquire in Your presence. Waiting patiently for a marriage partner has become a challenge—a trial, sometimes leading to temptation. I am asking for Your help in developing patience, quietly entrusting my future to Your will. It is to You that I submit my desire to be married.

By Your grace I surrender my life—all my desires, all that I am, and all that I am not—to the control of the Holy Spirit Who produces this kind of fruit in me: love, joy, peace, *patience,* kindness, goodness, faithfulness, gentleness, and self-control; and here there is no conflict. I belong to Jesus Christ, and I seek to live by the Holy Spirit's power and to follow the Holy Spirit's leading in every part of my life. [In exercising] self-control I [develop] steadfastness (patience, endurance), and in [exercising] steadfastness I [develop] godliness (piety).

By faith, I consider it wholly joyful whenever I am enveloped in, or encounter, trials of any sort or fall into various temptations. It is then that I am reminded to rest assured and understand that the trial and proving of my faith brings out endurance and steadfastness and patience. I purpose to let endurance and steadfastness and patience have full play and do a thorough work, so that I may be perfectly and fully developed [with no defects], lacking in nothing.

Father, fill me with the knowledge of Your will through all spiritual wisdom and understanding. Then I will live a life worthy of You and will please You in every way: bearing fruit in every good work. I ask You to help me grow in the knowledge of You, so that I might be strengthened with all power according to Your glorious might. Then I know that I will have great endurance and patience, and I will joyfully give thanks to You. I thank You for qualifying me to share in the inheritance of the saints in the Kingdom of light.

Father, I strip off and throw aside every encumbrance (unnecessary weight) and that sin which so readily (deftly and cleverly) clings to and entangles me, and I run with patient endurance and steady and active persistence the appointed course of the race that is set before me. I look away [from all that will distract] to Jesus, Who is the Leader and the Source of my faith [giving the first incentive for my belief] and is also its Finisher [bringing it to maturity and perfection].

With patience I am able to persevere through the difficult times—times of anxiety and worry—and overcome the fear that I may never be married. I am an overcomer by the blood of the Lamb and by the word of my testimony.

In Jesus' name, amen.

Scripture References

Psalm 27:4,8 AMP

Psalm 3:4 AMP

Psalm 37:4,5

Galatians 5:22-25 TLB

2 Peter 1:6 AMP

James 1:2-4 AMP

Colossians 1:9-12 NIV

Hebrews 12:1,2 AMP

Revelation 12:11

To Discipline in Love

Thank You for loving me, Father. Your love that is shed abroad in my heart enables me to discipline my children in love. I desire to imitate You, mimic Your speech and manner of life, just as well-behaved children imitate their parents. Thank You for sending the Holy Spirit to teach me to walk in love and in the light, and I pray that in our home I will walk circumspectly. I would imitate Your acts, words, nature, ways, graces, and Spirit. I pray that I will be alert, taking every opportunity to nurture, train, educate, discipline, and correct my children with love and praise.[11]

I purpose to discipline my children while there is hope, before their habits are formed and sealed for life, and I will not let my soul spare for their crying. I love my children too much to allow them to follow the customs and practices of this world. May I remember that it is better for them to cry now than for both of us to cry later.[12]

In the name of Jesus, I thank You for loving me so much that You do not allow me to continue in sin, but rather You chasten me; I will never grow weary of Your correction. In the name of Jesus, I resist fear; instead, I declare and decree that my children will not faint when I

[11] Based on study notes from Finis Jennings Dake, *Dake's Annotated Reference Bible* (Lawrenceville, Georgia: Dake Publishing, Inc., 2002), pp. 9. 369, 371, S.V. "Ephesians 5:1,16" and "Ephesians 6:4."

[12] Ibid, p. 1065, S.V. "Proverbs 3:11-12."

reprimand them. I am not in this alone, Holy Spirit; You are helping me convict and convince them of sin, righteous, and judgment so that they may walk in truth. I purpose to train my children, without seeking revenge; instead, I will correct them with loving concern. I will nourish them with wholesome discipline and instruction, which will bend them toward You, my Lord and my God.

Father, I pray that Christ may dwell in my heart through faith. And I pray that I, being rooted and established in love, may have power, together with all the saints, to grasp how wide and long and high and deep is the love of Christ, and to know this love that surpasses knowledge—that I may be filled to the measure of all Your fullness.

Your love in me enables me to be patient and kind. If I discipline my children, but have not love, it profits us nothing, and neither of us gain anything. My love will protect, trust, hope, and persevere. Love never fails. Thank You for being a father/mother to my children. My help comes from You, my Father and my God.

In Jesus' name, amen.

Scripture References

Romans 5:5

Ephesians 5:1,8,10,15 AMP

Proverbs 19:18

Proverbs 3:11,12

Hebrews 12:5

John 16:7,8

Ephesians 6:4

Proverbs 22:6 AMP

Ephesians 3:17-19 NIV

1 Corinthians 13:1-8

For Respecting Each Other

Father, this is an area of my life in which I need healing and restoration. The mistakes that I made before and after my children were born have stripped me of self-respect. How can I teach my children respect if I am not modeling it in front of them? Today I make a decision to forgive everyone who has wronged me. They could never repay what I believe they have stolen from me. *(Determine what you feel has been taken from you, let it go, and trust God.)* In the name of Jesus, I repent of and renounce all resentment and bitterness, and I stop it from controlling my children or me.

Father, I receive Your forgiveness, and I forgive myself for the sins and mistakes of the past. This day I reclaim my self-respect because I am Your child, and my sins are forgiven. I come with clean hands and a pure heart asking You to let me see my children as a heritage from You.

Oh, my Father, I am the elder, the voice of authority, in my home. Give me the vision of caring for the children You have entrusted to me. Create in me a willing heart to watch over them, not for what they can do for me, but because I am eager to serve You. I would not lord it over the children You have assigned to my care, but I vow to lead them by my good example. And when You, the head

Shepherd, come, my reward will be a never-ending share in Your glory and honor.

It is my desire that my children will honor and respect those who are over them in the Lord, admonishing and loving them. They will hold authority figures in the highest regard in love because of their work, and we will live in peace with each other.

In my heart I set apart Christ as Lord. May I always be prepared to give an answer to my children when they ask me to give them reasons, and I pray that I will do so with gentleness and respect, keeping a clear conscience. I purpose to listen to my children, praise them, and treat them with respect.

As a human father/mother, I will discipline them, and know that they will respect me for it. This will prepare them to submit to You, their heavenly Father, and live. Later on, it will produce a harvest of righteousness and peace for my children who have been trained by it.

As they walk in self-respect with a right attitude toward their father/mother, they will honor both their father and their mother, as You, the Lord our God, have commanded, so that they may live long and that it may go well with them.

Father, thank You for being a mother/father to my children who respect a command, and they will be rewarded.

In Jesus' name, amen.

Scripture References

Psalm 127:3 NIV

1 Peter 5:1-4 NLT

1 Thessalonians 5:12,13 NIV

1 Peter 3:15,16 NIV

Hebrews 12:9-11 NIV

Deuteronomy 5:16 NIV

Proverbs 13:13 NIV

For a Godly Support System (Through Church or Other God-Appointed Relationships)

Father, thank You for leading us to a church where Your truth, love, mercy, and grace are preached and practiced. Give me the courage to make the first move to reach out to others who are in need. You meet my need for support through my church, through God-appointed relationships, through individuals, and through groups* who are working on problem situations similar to mine.

When no one is available, I remember, Father, that You reached down from on high and drew me out of deep waters. You rescued me from my enemies (satanic forces), who were too strong for me. They confronted me in the day of my disaster, but You, Lord, were my support. You brought me out into a spacious place; You rescued me because You delighted in me.

---

* "A group is a community for its members. This community must be kept focused on what is encouraging, uplifting, and positive. Everybody should aim at learning the truth and applying it to life situations, resolving conflicts, and developing workable solutions to problems. Obedience to the truth should be stressed so that truth is not merely grasped intellectually but acted out in life. Support for a life of praise and obedience, bringing joy and peace, ought to be the focus of the group's existence." William Backus, *The Healing Power of a Christian Mind* (Minneapolis: Bethany House Publishers, 1996), p. 151.

Lord, You always answer me when I am in distress; the name of the God of Jacob protects me. Thank You for sending me help from the sanctuary and for granting me support from Zion. I submit to the God-appointed leaders in the church where my children and I are planted. We receive wisdom, guidance, and advice from them. Thank You for godly male/female mentors who are interested in supporting my children and me.

You, my Lord, see us. You formed the hearts of all, and You consider everything we do. Our hope is in Your unfailing love, to deliver us from death and keep us alive in famine. We wait in hope for You; You are our Help and our Shield. In You our hearts rejoice, for we trust in Your holy name.

When I said, "My foot is slipping," Your love, O Lord, supported me. When anxiety was great within me, Your consolation brought joy to my soul. So I will not fear, for You are with me; I will not be dismayed, for You are my God. You are strengthening me, helping me, and upholding me with Your righteous right hand as I train up my children in the way they should go. When I was lost You brought me back. I thank You for binding up our injuries and strengthening us. You will shepherd us with justice.

When I was being sifted as wheat, You prayed that my faith would not fail. Now that I have turned back to You, I will strengthen my brothers and sisters, giving those in my support group encouragement to remain true to the faith. We are mutually encouraged by each other's faith, building each other up, and encouraging each other to be self-controlled. Our love for one another gives us great joy and encouragement, because our hearts are refreshed.

Each member of our support group has made a commitment to encourage one another daily, as long as it is called Today, so that none of us may be hardened by sin's deceitfulness. We have come to share in Christ, if we hold firmly till the end the confidence we had at first. We will not give up meeting together, as some are in the habit of doing, but will continue to encourage one another—and all the more so as we see the Day is approaching. With the help of the Holy Spirit, Who is our Strengthener and Standby, and in the name of Jesus, we offer this prayer. Amen.

Scripture References

2 Samuel 22:17-20 NIV

Psalm 20:1,2 NIV

Psalm 33:13-21 NIV

Psalm 94:18,19 NIV

Isaiah 41:10 NIV

Proverbs 22:6

Ezekiel 34:16 NIV

Luke 22:31,32 NIV

Acts 14:21,22 NIV

Romans 1:12 NIV

Proverbs 11:25 NIV

Romans 15:4-6

1 Thessalonians 5:11 NIV

Titus 2:6 NIV

Hebrews 3:13,14 NIV

Hebrews 10:25 NIV

John 14:16 AMP

To Have the Answers to the Questions Your Children Ask

O, my Father, I come into Your throne room asking for mercy and grace. Behold, You desire truth in the inward parts; in the hidden part You will make me to know wisdom. Your wisdom will enable me to be straight-forward, answering my children's questions openly and honestly in love. The truth will set us free.

O Lord, God of Abraham, Isaac, and Israel, let it be known today that You are God in our home, and that I am Your servant. Answer me, O Lord; answer me, so that my children will know that You, O Lord, are God. I pray that my children will know and proclaim, "The Lord—He is God! The Lord—He is God!" (1 Kings 18:39 NIV).

My children are distressed about the absence of their father/mother. Lord, help me answer them and give them assurance that You will protect them. Deliver them from shame and condemnation for living in a single-parent home. They are not responsible for the mistakes we (their parents) have made. I will answer wisely, restraining my lips, for in the multitude of words sin is not lacking.

Thank You for Your grace, which is sufficient to give me a gentle answer that turns away wrath. As a man/woman in right standing with You, I will weigh my answers. My conversation will be full of grace, seasoned with salt, so that I may know how to answer my children with gentleness. It is in the name of Jesus that I pray. Amen.

Scripture References

Psalm 51:6 NKJV

1 Kings 18:36-39 NIV

Psalm 20:1

Proverbs 10:19 NKJV

Proverbs 15:1 NKJV

Proverbs 15:28 NIV

Colossians 4:6 NIV

For Good Communication
With Your Children

Father, I recognize that good communication with my children begins with me. Give me wisdom to help them process their anger and guilt and to speak words that will bring healing.

In the name of Jesus, I have resolved that my mouth will not sin. Father, I realize that above all else, I must guard my heart, for it affects everything I do. I pray that the words of my mouth and the meditation of my heart may be pleasing in Your sight, O Lord, my Rock and my Redeemer. My mouth will speak words of wisdom; the utterance from my heart will give understanding when I converse with my children.

Father, You are my Help, and I pray that You will set a guard over my mouth, O Lord; keep watch over the door of my lips. I will be wise and listen when my children speak, and add to their learning, and I purpose to walk in discernment and receive guidance.

Give my children a listening heart that they may receive instruction and not forsake their father's/mother's teaching. As we talk, we will listen to each other so that we may live in safety and be at ease, without fear of harm.

In the name of Jesus, I bind my mind to the mind of Christ, and my emotions to the control of the Holy Spirit. I loose wrong attitudes, and negative, ungodly thought patterns from our minds. Give us listening hearts and ears to hear the voice of our God and each other. May I teach my children by precept and practice to guard their mouths and their tongues to keep them from calamity. I will teach them that there is a time to be silent and a time to speak.

For though we walk in the flesh, we do not war according to the flesh. For the weapons of our warfare are not carnal but mighty in You for pulling down strong-holds, casting down arguments and every high thing that exalts itself against the knowledge of You, Lord, bringing every thought into captivity to the obedience of Christ. We will think on good things and store up good things in our hearts, for out of the overflow of our hearts our mouths speak.

Therefore grant us grace that we may put off false-hood and speak truthfully to each other, for we are all members of one body. In our anger we will not sin; we take a stand that we will not let the sun go down while we are still angry. We refuse to give the devil a foothold, in the name of Jesus. We rid ourselves of all bitterness, rage and anger, brawling and slander, along with every form of malice. With the help of the Holy Spirit my children and

I will be kind and compassionate to one another, forgiving each other, just as in Christ You forgave us.

Thank You, Father, for loving us. Amen.

Scripture References

Psalm 17:3 NIV

Proverbs 4:23 NLT

Psalm 19:14 NIV

Psalm 49:3 NIV

Psalm 141:3 NKJV

Proverbs 1:5 NIV

Proverbs 1:8 NIV

Proverbs 1:33 NIV

Proverbs 21:23 NIV

Ecclesiastes 3:7 NIV

Luke 6:43-45

2 Corinthians 10:3-5 NKJV

Philippians 4:8

Matthew 12:34 NIV

Ephesians 4:25-27 NIV

Ephesians 4:31,32 NIV

Your Children's Direction for Life

Father, as I train up my children according to Your ways, I believe that they will dedicate themselves to live for You. They won't know everything the future holds for them, but they will know that it is in Your hands. They will trust You to lead them and to be their guide in life. Lord, I trust You to prepare my children now for Your life plan for them. Thank You that they will have the wisdom to discern the right timing for what You would have them do in each season of their life. They will choose to love, obey, and cleave unto You with their whole body, soul, and spirit.

If college is in their future, please help them to select the right one. Thank You for providing the means for them to go. If it is not college, then prepare them for their job. Help them to recognize the skills You have given them so that they can develop those skills and give the glory to You. Give them understanding and light so that they are quick to learn. Thank You for the wisdom and light that come from You and Your Word.

I believe that my children depend on You to be a help to them in everything they do. If it is Your will for them to marry someday, thank You that You are not only preparing them, but that You are also working on their future spouse. Until that time comes, help them to be content in every situation.

They will depend upon You to provide for them—that You will supply all the money they need to do Your will. They will believe You to instruct and teach them which way to go. They will trust that You won't make things confusing for them, but that You will make a clear path for them when they put You first.

Thank You that my children will read and meditate on Your words, which are a light for their path. Thank You for Your Holy Spirit Who will reveal to them Your plan for them. I believe my children treasure their life with and for You. Thank You, Father, for holding my children's future in the palm of Your hand.

In Jesus' name I pray, amen.

Scripture References

1 Corinthians 2:9,10

John 16:13

Ephesians 2:10

Deuteronomy 30:20

Ephesians 1:16-18

1 Peter 5:7

Ecclesiastes 3:1-8

Hebrews 13:5

Philippians 4:11,13,19

Proverbs 22:6

Proverbs 3:5,6

Psalm 32:8

Psalm 25:5

Proverbs 4:18

Jeremiah 33:3

Romans 8:14

Psalm 119:105

Isaiah 49:16

To Discuss Remarriage With Your Children

Introduction

There are very few Scriptures dealing with remarriage—in order to discuss this subject with your children, you need wisdom, answers for their questions, and good communication skills. I encourage you to pray the previous prayers and meditate on the Scriptures listed. Praying scriptural prayers will prepare you to deal with issues that are very real. I encourage you to gather information that will give you insight and wisdom.

Prayer does not relieve you of the responsibility of learning all you can about the issues you will be facing, but it does prepare your heart and mind to resolve conflicts and issues as they arise. Give this prayer and the previous prayers place in your thoughts, because this is a traumatic event in the lives of your children.[14]

Seek wise counsel for yourself, your fiancé(e), and your children: "Wisdom is the principal thing; therefore get wisdom. And in all your getting, get understanding"

---

[14] "Along with the dream of living in a two-parent home, every child of divorce clings to the dream that the natural parents will somehow reunite. When the mom or dad remarries, that effectively destroys the dream of reunion." Dr. Frank Minirty, Dr. Brian Newman, and Dr. Paul Warren, *The Father Book: An Instruction Manual* (Nashville, TN: Thomas Nelson, Inc., 1992), p. 239.

(Prov. 4:7 NKJV). I encourage you to read 1 Corinthians 7 and ask the Holy Spirit to give you insight as you ponder Paul's discussion of marriage and remarriage.

Prayer

Holy Spirit, before I talk with my children about remarriage, search our hearts, for You know what the mind of the Spirit is, because You make intercession for us according to the will of God. And I know that all things work together for good to those who love God, to those who are the called according to His purpose.

Father, after my divorce I felt as though I had been carried into exile, but You healed me and brought me back to You with cords and bands of unconditional love. My heart has grown content, but now I believe that it is Your plan for me to remarry. My children and I will go out with joy, and will be led out with peace. The mountains and the hills will break forth into singing before us, and all the trees of the field will clap their hands.

Go before our discussion and prepare my children's hearts to hear. O Lord, give them a heart to understand, and give me the wisdom that I may choose my words wisely.

In the name of Jesus, I have made my plans, but from You, Lord, comes the wise reply of the tongue. Father, thank You for feeding me like a shepherd, and

for gathering my children and me with Your arm,
carrying us in Your bosom, and gently leading me as I
discuss remarriage with them.

In the name of Jesus, I present this request. Amen.

Scripture References

Proverbs 4:7 NKJV   Isaiah 55:12 NKJV

1 Corinthians 7:1-39 NIV   Proverbs 16:1 NIV

Romans 8:27,28 NKJV   Isaiah 40:11 NKJV

Hosea 11:4

To Operate in Discernment

Introduction

Many times in the Bible God revealed things to people. We see this in Daniel 2:19, Jeremiah 11:18, and 1 Samuel 3:21. God is no respecter of persons (Acts 10:34), which means that He will give you discernment, insight, and revelation in the same way as you raise your children in the nurture and admonition of the Lord (Eph. 6:4).

Prayer

Oh, my Father, I am Your servant; give me discernment that I may understand Your statutes and teach them diligently to my children. And this is my prayer: that my love may abound more and more in knowledge and depth of insight, so that I may be able to discern what is best and may be pure and blameless until the day of Christ, filled with the fruit of righteousness that comes through Jesus Christ—to the glory and praise of You, my God. As I reflect on Your Word, You will give me insight into all this.

Thank You for discernment that enables me to see that which is hidden. I praise You, Father, Lord of heaven and earth, because You give me needed revelation. I resist the spirit of fear, and will not be afraid. There is nothing concealed that will not be disclosed, or hidden that will not be made known.

The Spirit of Christ abides in me, and I realize that the things of God are revealed to me by the Spirit and that they are spiritually discerned. Therefore, I continue to ask You, the God of our Lord Jesus Christ, the glorious Father, to give me the Spirit of wisdom and revelation, so that I may know You better. I pray also that the eyes of my heart may be enlightened in order that I may know the hope to which You have called me, the riches of Your glorious inheritance in the saints, and Your incomparably great power for us who believe.

In the name of Jesus I will listen and add to my learning, and as I discern I will receive guidance. I preserve sound judgment and discernment; I will not let them out of my sight; they will be life for me, an ornament to grace my neck. Then I will go on my way in safety, and my foot will not stumble; when I lie down, I will not be afraid and my sleep will be sweet. I declare and decree that I am discerning, and my pleasant words promote instruction.

It is in the name of Jesus that I pray. Amen.

Scripture References

Psalm 119:125 NIV

Philippians 1:9-11 NIV

Proverbs 28:11 NIV

Luke 10:21 NIV

2 Timothy 2:7 NIV

Matthew 10:26 NIV

Romans 8:9 NIV

1 Corinthians 2:6-14 NIV

Ephesians 1:17 NIV

Proverbs 1:5 NIV

Proverbs 3:21-24 NIV

Proverbs 16:21 NIV

Part VIII

Prayers for
Your Children

For Your Children

Father, in the name of Jesus, I pray for my children and confess Your Word over them, surrounding them with my faith—faith in Your Word that You watch over it to perform it! I confess and believe that my children are disciples of Christ, [taught by You and obedient to Your will]. Great is the peace and undisturbed composure of my children, because You, God, contend with that which contends with them, and You give them safety and ease them.

Father, You will perfect that which concerns me and my children. *I commit and cast the care of my children once and for all on You, Father.* They are in Your hands, and I am [positively] persuaded that You are able to guard and keep that which I have committed [to You]. You are more than enough!

I confess that my children obey their parents in the Lord [as Your representatives], because this is just and right. My children honor (esteem and value as precious) their parents—for this is the first commandment with a promise: that all may be well with my children and that they may live long on the earth. I believe and confess that my children choose life and love You, Lord, that they obey Your voice and cling to You; for You are their life and the length of their days. Therefore, my children are the head and not the tail, and they shall be above only and not beneath. They are blessed when they come in, and when they go out.

I believe and confess that You give Your angels charge over my children to accompany and defend and preserve them in all their ways. You, Lord, are their Refuge and Fortress. You are their Glory and the Lifter of their heads.

As a parent, I will not provoke, irritate, or fret my children. I will not [be hard on them or harass them] or cause them to become discouraged, sullen, or morose, or to feel inferior and frustrated. [I will not break or wound their spirits], but I will rear them [tenderly] in the training, discipline, counsel, and admonition of the Lord. I will train them in the way they should go, and when they are old, they will not depart from it.

O Lord, my Lord, how excellent (majestic and glorious) is Your name in all the earth! You have set Your glory on [or above] the heavens. Out of the mouth of babes and unweaned infants You have established strength because of Your foes, that You might silence the enemy and the avenger. I sing praises to Your name, O Most High. *The enemy is turned back from my children in the name of Jesus!* They increase in wisdom and in favor with You and man. Amen.

Scripture References

Jeremiah 1:12 AMP

Isaiah 54:13 AMP

Isaiah 49:25 AMP

Psalm 138:8 AMP

1 Peter 5:7 AMP

2 Timothy 1:12 AMP

Psalm 4:6 MESSAGE

Ephesians 6:1-3 AMP

Deuteronomy 30:19,20 AMP

Deuteronomy 28:13 AMP

Psalm 91:11 AMP

Psalm 91:2 AMP

Psalm 3:3 AMP

Colossians 3:21 AMP

Ephesians 6:4 AMP

Proverbs 22:6 AMP

Psalm 8:1,2 AMP

Psalm 9:2,3 AMP

Luke 2:52 AMP

Deuteronomy 28:6 AMP

Restoration of Your Children's Mind, Will, and Emotions

Father, my children and I have seen troubles, many and bitter, and I ask You to restore our lives again; from the depths of the earth bring us up. Restore us, O God, and make Your face shine upon us, that we may be saved.

Lord Jesus, I believe that You are able to restore my children to emotional wholeness, and I cry from the depths of my being, "Have mercy on my children, Son of David!" (Matt. 9:27 NIV). Lord, You are called the Repairer of Broken Walls, Restorer of Streets with Dwellings. I purpose to rebuild the ruins, and You will restore us to health and heal our wounds.

Thank You for hearing my prayer, and watching over Your Word to perform it on behalf of my children. I trust You to restore them to soundness and emotional health. Surely it was for my benefit that I suffered such anguish, and I ask You to use it for good and not evil in the lives of my children. In Your love You have kept my children from the pit of destruction; You have put all their sins behind Your back. I pray that they will not suffer for the sins of their parents.

In the name of Jesus, I pray that my children and I will be free from rejection, resentment, envy, jealousy, and anger. Christ, You have really set us free. Now we want to make sure that we stay free, resisting the negative thoughts and feelings that would enslave us again. When my ex-spouse is doing well financially and establishing new relationships, give us the grace to rejoice.

God of all grace, You called us to Your eternal glory in Christ. After we have suffered a little while, You will restore us and make us strong, firm, and steadfast. Thank You for loving us, in the name of Jesus. Amen.

Scripture References

Psalm 71:20 NIV

Psalm 80:3 NIV

Matthew 9:27 NIV

Isaiah 58:12 NIV

Jeremiah 30:17,18

Psalm 23:3 NIV

Jeremiah 1:12 AMP

Isaiah 38:16,17 NIV

Amos 5:14 NLT

Galatians 5:1 NLT

1 Peter 5:10 NIV

Your Children's Relationships

Father, I pray for my children that they will have favor with You and with all men. I pray that they will keep Your laws and obey Your commands. I pray that they will remember to be truthful and kind from deep within their hearts; then they will find favor with both You and man. I pray that they will acquire a reputation for good judgment and common sense.

Father, in the name of Jesus, You make Your face to shine upon and enlighten my children and are gracious (kind, merciful, and giving favor) to them. They are the head and not the tail, above only and not beneath.

Because they seek Your Kingdom and Your righteousness, and diligently seek good, they produce favor. They are a blessing to You, Lord, and a blessing to _____ *(name them: family members, neighbors, school mates, friends, teachers, etc.)*. Grace (favor) is with them because they love the Lord Jesus in sincerity. You extend favor, honor, and love to them so that they are always flowing in Your love, Father. You are pouring out upon them the Spirit of favor. You crown them with glory and honor for they are Your children—Your workmanship.

They are a success today. Each of them is someone very special to You, Lord. They are growing in You— waxing strong in spirit. Father, You give them knowledge and skill in all learning and wisdom. You bring them to find favor, compassion, and loving-kindness with everyone. They obtain favor in the sight of all who look upon them this day, in the name of Jesus. They are filled with Your fullness—rooted and grounded in love. You are doing exceeding abundantly above all that I ask or think, for Your mighty power is taking over in them.

Thank You, Father, that my children are well-favored by You and by man.

In Jesus' name I pray, amen.

Scripture References

Luke 2:52 AMP

Proverbs 3:1-4 TLB

Numbers 6:25 AMP

Deuteronomy 28:13 AMP

Matthew 6:33 AMP

Proverbs 11:27 AMP

Ephesians 6:24 AMP

Esther 2:15,17

Psalm 118:25 AMP

Zechariah 2:8 NLT

Zechariah 12:10 AMP

Psalm 8:5 AMP

Ephesians 2:10 AMP

Luke 2:40

Daniel 1:17,9 AMP

Ephesians 3:19,20 KJV

For Your Children's Future

Father, Your Word declares that children are an inheritance from You and promises peace when they are taught in Your ways. I dedicate _____ to You today, that he/she may be raised as You desire and will follow the path You choose. Father, I confess Your Word this day over _____. I thank You that Your Word goes out and will not return unto You void, but will accomplish what You send it to do.

Heavenly Father, I commit myself, as a parent, to train _____ in the way he/she should go, trusting in the promise that he/she will not depart from Your ways, but will grow and prosper in them. I turn the care and burden of raising him/her over to You. I will not provoke my child, but I will nurture and leave him/her in Your care. I will do as Your Word commands and teach my child diligently. My child will be upon my heart and mind. Your grace is sufficient to overcome my inabilities as a parent.

My child _____ is obedient and honors both his/her parents, being able to accept the abundant promises of Your Word of long life and prosperity. _____ is a godly child, not ashamed or afraid to honor and keep Your Word. He/she stands convinced that You are the Almighty God. I am thankful that as _____ grows, he/she will remember You and not pass by the opportunity of a relationship with Your Son, Jesus. Your great blessings will be upon _____ for keeping Your ways. I thank You for Your blessings over every area of _____'s life, that You will see to the salvation and obedience of his/her life to Your ways.

Heavenly Father, I thank You now that laborers will be sent into _____'s path, preparing the way for salvation, as it is written in Your Word, through Your Son, Jesus. I am thankful that _____ will recognize the devices of the devil and will be delivered to salvation through the purity of Your Son. You have given _____ the grace and the strength to walk the narrow pathway to Your Kingdom.

I pray that just as Jesus increased in wisdom and stature, so this child will be blessed with the same wisdom and stature, and that You will pour out Your favor and blessings openly on him/her.

I praise You in advance for _____'s future spouse. Father, Your Word declares that You desire for Your children to be pure and honorable, waiting upon marriage. I speak blessings to the future union and believe that _____ will be well suited to his/her partner and that their household will be in godly order, holding fast to the love of Jesus Christ. Continue to prepare _____ to be the man/woman of God that You desire him/her to be.

_____ will be diligent and hard-working, never lazy or undisciplined. Your Word promises great blessing to his/her house, and he/she shall always be satisfied and will always increase. Godliness is profitable unto his/her house, and _____ shall receive the promise of life and all that is to come.

Father, thank You for protecting and guiding my child.

In Jesus' name I pray, amen.

Scripture References

Psalm 127:3	2 Timothy 2:26
Isaiah 54:13	Job 22:30
Isaiah 55:11	Matthew 7:14
Proverbs 22:6	Luke 2:52
1 Peter 5:7	Hebrews 13:4 NIV
Ephesians 6:4	1 Thessalonians 4:3
Deuteronomy 6:7	Ephesians 5:22-25 NIV
2 Corinthians 12:9	2 Timothy 1:13
Ephesians 6:1-3	Proverbs 13:11
Proverbs 8:17,32	Proverbs 20:13 NKJV
Luke 19:10	Romans 12:11
Matthew 9:38	1 Timothy 4:8 NIV
2 Corinthians 2:11	Psalm 91:1,11

For Your Children
in Different Stages of Adolescence

Introduction

A single mother whose children are now adults wrote:

"I prayed Romans 8:28 over so many situations with
the thought that God was not surprised by my husband's
decision to leave. I chose to believe that God formed my
children with that fact in mind; thus they had everything,
every grace, they needed built in ahead of time to come
out of all of this with what God had planned for them in
the Kingdom intact. Many times our holidays looked very
different from family, friends, or the other parent. I prayed
for divinely inspired new traditions and miraculous provision. God always answered, many times with simplicity,
and the children knew Christmas was a gift from God."

This mother's testimony reveals the power of prayer
and ministry to her children. In the midst of their trouble,
God preserved their lives, and with His right hand He
saved them (Ps. 138:7 NIV).

She wrote: "Forgiveness is a huge issue for prayer,
forgiving the former spouse, friends, family, and those
who just don't understand, even at church. The children
encountered rejection and persecution from teachers,

neighbors, and friends, even at our church. We focused on who we are in Christ.

"One time at church my daughter (after a sermon on fatherless America) handed me a note that read, 'Mom, I am not fatherless—the Creator of the universe is my Father.' Her father sees my son but has never spoken to her since the divorce. God, however, is more than enough."

Prayer

Father of all comfort, when my children are reminded by church or school events that they are living in a single-parent home, I ask You to release Your anointing to bind up and heal their broken hearts. Thank You for Your anointing that breaks every yoke of bondage. The chastisement [needful to obtain] peace and well-being for us was upon You, my Kinsman-Redeemer, and with the stripes [that wounded] You we are healed and made whole.

Father, my children will not have to drink from my cup of sorrow, because You have turned my sorrow into joy! You took away my clothes of mourning and clothed me with joy. You have delivered me from a spirit of fear and given me a spirit of power, love, and a sound mind. Holy Spirit, I ask You to reveal my children's passion for life and their divine call. For they are Your workmanship, created in Christ Jesus for good works, which You, Father, prepared beforehand that they should walk in them. Their security and future are founded in You.

Lord, create in my children a heart of trust in their loving heavenly Father Who will never leave them or forsake them. As we develop new inspiring, fun holiday traditions, we look to You, *El-Shaddi*, God Almighty (Ex. 6:3 AMP), for miraculous provision.

You are effectually at work in my children [energizing and creating in them both the will and the desire] to please You. Help them forgive everyone who does not understand, and give them the grace to resist the temptation to receive rejection and self-pity.

I come before You asking You—the God of our Master, Jesus Christ, the God of glory—to make my children intelligent and discerning in knowing You personally. Give them understanding and open their eyes when viewing this whole single-parent situation, and close their eyes when it is necessary to protect and guard their hearts and innocence. Keep their eyes focused and clear, so that they can see exactly what it is You are calling them to do. Manifest Yourself to my children, speak to them so they understand and know that they are loved with a pure, unconditional love. You are a father/mother to them.

Father, You have given me the ministry of reconciliation [that by word and deed I might aim to bring my children in harmony with You]. I ask for Your wisdom in all situations that I might be Your true representative. I weep with my children in their sorrow and disappointment, and I rejoice with them in their victories. Father, I have no greater joy than to hear that my children are walking in the truth.

I offer this prayer in the precious name of Jesus. Amen.

Scripture References

Isaiah 61:1

Isaiah 10:27

Isaiah 53:5 AMP

Ruth 3:9 NIV

Psalm 30:11 TLB

2 Timothy 1:7

Ephesians 2:10 NKJV

Hebrews 13:5

Philippians 4:19

Philippians 2:13 AMP

Ephesians 1:17-19 MESSAGE

2 Corinthians 5:18,20 AMP

Romans 12:15 AMP

3 John 4

For Your Children's Wise Choice of Friends

Father, I come boldly to Your throne of grace to ask You to help my children to meet some new friends. I know that You are the Source of love and friendship, but that You also desire to express Your love and friendship toward my children through others. So, I am convinced that it is Your will for my children to have godly friendships with members of both sexes.

Your Word reveals the purpose and value of healthy friendships. It is not the quantity, but the quality of friends that matters.

Holy Spirit, teach my children what they need to know to be a quality friend. Help them to show themselves friendly to others and to love their friends at all times. Help them to purpose to live in peace as much as is possible. I pray that when they and their friends come together, they will encourage each other. Help them to rid themselves of any prejudice or partiality. I pray that they will not [attempt to] hold [and] practice the faith of our Lord Jesus Christ [the Lord] of glory [together with snobbery]! Instead, they will welcome and receive others as You, Father, have received them.

Help them to be kind, humble, and gentle, and to forgive those who need forgiveness, because they are forgiven.

I pray that they and their new friends will be in perfect harmony and full agreement and that there will be no dissentions or factions or divisions among them, but that they will be perfectly united. Help them to stand firm in a united spirit and be of a single mind and one in purpose and intention, their hearts knit together in love. May their love for one another be so strong that, as the Lord Jesus did, they will feel that they would be willing to lay down their very lives for one another.

For my children's new friends, I thank You.

In Jesus' name I pray, amen.

Scripture References

Hebrews 4:16	James 2:1 AMP
James 1:17	Romans 15:7 AMP
Psalm 84:11	Ephesians 4:2,32 AMP
Ecclesiastes 4:9,10	1 Corinthians 1:10 AMP
Proverbs 13:20	Philippians 1:27 AMP
Proverbs 18:24	Philippians 2:2 AMP
Proverbs 17:17	Colossians 2:2
Romans 12:18	John 15:13

Protection

Father, I am Your child. The blood of the Lamb has redeemed me, and my sins are forgiven.

As the head of my household, I pray according to Your Word, asking for Your protection for each of us. Give safety to my children and ease them day by day. Our life is exceedingly filled with the scorning and scoffing of those who are at ease and with the contempt of the proud (irresponsible tyrants who disregard Your law).

Lord, You see the violence that is in the streets and in our schools. The drug dealers and the gang members living in our neighborhoods are waiting to snare our children.

On the authority of Your Word, I ask that You destroy [their schemes]; O Lord, confuse their tongues, for I have seen violence and strife in the inner city. Day and night they go about on its walls; iniquity and mischief are in its midst. Violence and ruin are within it; fraud and guile do not depart from its streets and marketplaces. I am calling upon You, Lord, and You will save me and my household as well.

Father, You, and You alone, are our safety and our protection. My household and I are looking to You, for our strength comes from You—the God Who made heaven and earth. You will not let us stumble. You are our

Guardian God Who will not fall asleep. You are right at our side to protect us. You guard us from every evil; You guard our very lives. You guard us when we leave and when we return. You guard us now, and You will continue to guard us always.

My household was chosen and foreknown by You, Father, and consecrated (sanctified, made holy) by the Spirit to be obedient to Jesus Christ (the Messiah) and to be sprinkled with [His] blood. We receive grace (spiritual blessing) and peace in ever-increasing abundance [that spiritual peace to be realized in and through Christ, freedom from fears, agitating passions, and moral conflicts].

Lord, Your Son, Jesus, became our Passover by shedding His own precious blood. He is the Mediator (the Go-between, Agent) of a new covenant, and His sprinkled blood speaks of mercy. On the authority of Your Word, I proclaim that the blood of Jesus is our protection; as You have said in Your Word, "When I see the blood, I will pass over you" (Ex. 12:13 AMP). I declare and decree that I am drawing a bloodline around my children, and the evil one cannot cross it.

I know that none of the God-begotten make a practice of sin—fatal sin. The God-begotten are also the God-protected. The evil one can't lay a hand on my household. I know that we are held firm by You, Lord.

Father, thank You for Your divine protection. In the name of Jesus I pray, amen.*

Scripture References

1 John 3:1	Psalm 121:1-8 MESSAGE
1 Peter 1:18,19	1 Peter 1:2 AMP
1 John 2:12	1 Corinthians 5:7 AMP
Psalm 123:4 AMP	Hebrews 12:24 AMP
Psalm 55:9-11,16 AMP	1 John 5:18,19 MESSAGE

---

* In addition to praying this prayer, read Psalm 91 aloud over your family each day.

Peaceful Sleep

Father, thank You for peaceful sleep, and for Your angels that encamp around us who fear You. You deliver us and keep us safe. The angels excel in strength, do Your commandments, and heed the voice of Your Word. You give Your angels charge over us, to keep us in all our ways.

We bring every thought, every imagination, and every dream into the captivity and obedience of Jesus Christ. Father, I thank You that, even as my children and I sleep, our heart counsels us and reveals to us Your purpose and plan for us. Thank You for sweet sleep, for You promised Your beloved sweet sleep. Therefore, our heart is glad, and our spirit rejoices. Our body and soul rest and confidently dwell in safety, amen.

Scripture References

Psalm 34:7 AMP	Proverbs 3:24
Psalm 103:20	Psalm 16:7-9 AMP
Psalm 91:11	Psalm 127:2
2 Corinthians 10:5	Psalm 4:8

The School Systems
Your Children Attend

Father, I thank You that the entrance of Your Word brings light and that You watch over Your Word to perform it. I bring before You the school system(s) my children attend and the men and women who are in positions of authority within it/them.

I ask You to give them skillful and godly wisdom, that Your knowledge might be pleasant to them. Then discretion will watch over them; understanding will keep them and deliver them from the way of evil and from evil people. I pray that men and women of integrity, blameless and complete [in Your sight], will remain in these positions, but that the wicked will be cut off and the treacherous will be rooted out in the name of Jesus. I thank You for placing born-again, Spirit-filled people in these positions.

Father, I bring my children before You. I speak forth Your Word boldly and confidently, Father, that I and the members of my household are saved in the name of Jesus. We are redeemed from the curse of the law, for Jesus was made a curse for us. *My sons and daughters are not given to another people.* I enjoy my children, and they will not go into captivity, in the name of Jesus.

As a single parent, I train my children in the way they should go, confident that when they are old they will not depart from it.

My children shrink from whatever might offend You and discredit the name of Christ. They show themselves to be blameless, guileless, innocent, and uncontaminated children of God, without blemish (faultless, unrebukable), in the midst of a crooked and wicked generation, holding out [to it] and offering [to all] the Word of Life. Thank You, Father, that You give them knowledge and skill in all learning and wisdom and bring them into favor with those around them.

Father, I pray and intercede that all the young people, their parents, and the leaders in the school system(s) will separate themselves from contact with contaminating and corrupting influences and will cleanse themselves from everything that would contaminate and defile their spirits, souls, and bodies. I confess that they shun immorality and all sexual looseness [flee from impurity in thought, word, or deed] and that they live and conduct themselves honorably and becomingly as in the [open light of] day. I confess and believe that they shun youthful lusts and flee from them in the name of Jesus.

Father, I ask You to commission the angels, Your ministering spirits, to go forth and police the area, dispelling the forces of darkness.

I thank You that in Christ all the treasures of [divine] wisdom (of comprehensive insight into Your ways and purposes) and [all the riches of spiritual] knowledge and enlightenment are stored up and lie hidden for my children, and that they walk in Him.

I praise You, Father, that I will see my children and all those in their school system [walking in the ways of piety and virtue], revering Your name. I pray that those who err in spirit will come to understanding, and that those who murmur [discontentedly] will accept instruction in the way, conforming to Your will and carrying out Your purposes in their lives. May You, Father, occupy first place in their hearts as I continue to surround all of them with my faith.

Thank You, Father, that You are the delivering God. Thank You that the good news of the Gospel is published throughout our school system(s). Thank You for intercessors to stand on Your Word and for laborers of the harvest to preach Your Word in Jesus' name.

Praise the Lord! Amen.

Scripture References

Psalm 119:130

Jeremiah 1:12 AMP

Proverbs 2:10-12 AMP

Proverbs 2:21,22 AMP

Acts 16:31

Galatians 3:13

Deuteronomy 28:32,41

Proverbs 22:6 AMP

Philippians 2:12,15,16 AMP

Daniel 1:17 AMP

Daniel 1:9

2 Timothy 2:21 AMP

2 Corinthians 7:1 AMP

1 Corinthians 6:18 AMP

Romans 13:13 AMP

2 Timothy 2:22 AMP

2 Timothy 2:26

Hebrews 1:14

Colossians 2:3 AMP

Isaiah 29:23,24 AMP

Matthew 9:38

1 John 2:16,17 AMP

For Children With Special Needs

Father, I come before You boldly and confidently, knowing that You watch over Your Word to perform it, just as You have performed miracles throughout history.

I pray for my children who have special needs, asking You to quicken them to Your Word—that they may be filled with wisdom and revelation knowledge concerning the integrity of Your Word. I pray for the infilling of the Holy Spirit, divine health, the fruit of the recreated human spirit, the gifts of the Holy Spirit, and deliverance. Lord, You are the Source of every consolation, comfort, and encouragement, and my children are to be sanctified in spirit, soul, and body.

I pray for deliverance of their bodies and minds, for You, Lord God, are the health of their countenance and the lifter of those bowed down—the joy of the Lord is their strength and stronghold! I ask You to commission ministering spirits to go forth as they hearken to Your Word to provide the necessary help for and assistance to those for whom I am praying.

Nothing is too hard or impossible for You. Because of our faith in You, all things are possible to us who believe. Let my prayers be set forth as incense before You—a sweet fragrance to You! Praise the Lord!

In the name of Jesus I pray, amen.

Scripture References

Hebrews 4:16 AMP

Jeremiah 1:12 AMP

Ephesians 1:17,18

Psalm 119:89 AMP

Ephesians 2:10 AMP

2 Corinthians 1:3 AMP

1 Thessalonians 5:23 AMP

Psalm 42:11

Psalm 145:14

Psalm 3:3 AMP

Nehemiah 8:10

Psalm 103:20

Luke 1:37 AMP

Mark 9:23 AMP

Psalm 141:2 AMP

Wisdom for Your Children in Daily Living

Heavenly Father, I pray that my children will be filled with the clear knowledge of Your will in all wisdom and understanding. I know that Your will and Your Word agree. I pray that my children will continue to meditate on Your Word so they can know Your plan and Your purpose for this season in their lives. I want them to live in a way that is worthy of You and fully pleasing to You. I believe You will cause their thoughts to agree with Your will so that they may be fruitful in every good work.

Your wisdom is pure and full of compassion. I ask that my children may develop in love and be strong in faith, knowing that Your words contain a wealth of wisdom. Whatever situations they may face in life, I thank You for Your wisdom so that they always know the right thing to do and say. Thank You that they have decided to listen to You. Teach them the way that You want them to go. Thank You for counseling them and watching carefully over them. Thank You for the Holy Spirit; He is their Teacher, Helper, and Guide, and I believe He is active in their lives.

My children will not be afraid or confused, because Your Word brings them light and understanding. Although there are many voices in the world, they will follow the voice of the Good Shepherd Who laid down His life for the sheep.

Thank You for the wise parents, teachers, and pastors You have placed in my children's lives. They are people You can use to teach and instruct them. I pray that they will seek godly counsel from them. When they need to make an important, final decision, I pray that they will follow the peace that comes from knowing Your Word.

I dedicate my children to You, knowing that their plans will succeed. I trust You with their lives and everything in them. I thank You that to follow after You is to follow after peace in their hearts. I thank You for Your wisdom that causes them to stand and to walk wisely, making the most of their time.

In Jesus' name I pray, amen.

Scripture References

Colossians 1:9 NIV

1 John 5:14,15 AMP

Joshua 1:8

Colossians 3:16

Colossians 1:10 AMP

Proverbs 16:3 AMP

Colossian 1:10

James 3:17 AMP

Philippians 1:9 AMP

Romans 4:20

James 1:5,6 AMP

Psalm 32:8 NIV

Psalm 16:7 AMP

John 14:26 AMP

1 Corinthians 14:33

Proverbs 6:20-23

John 10:1-5,15

Proverbs 2:6 AMP

Proverbs 16:3 NIV

Psalm 118:8 AMP

Hebrews 12:14

Psalm 119:99,130,133

Proverbs 19:21

Ephesians 5:15,16 NASB

To Discuss the Divorce, Separation, or Reason You Are Raising Your Children Alone

Introduction

God doesn't like divorce, but He loves divorced people. God doesn't like sexual immorality, but He loves unwed parents. Remember that the Father forgives (1 John 1:9), and that you are a new creation in Christ Jesus (2 Cor. 5:17 NKJV). God is merciful, and He is the God of the second chance: "Open up before God, keep nothing back; he'll do whatever needs to be done: He'll validate your life in the clear light of day and stamp you with approval at high noon" (Ps. 37:5,6 MESSAGE).

Put away bitterness, fear, and resentment. When talking with your children, do not allow yourself to blame others for what has happened to you. Admit where you were wrong or at fault, and be honest with yourself and them. Do not talk with scorn or disrespect about the one who is no longer in the home. When you talk with your children, speak the truth in love rather than tearing down and destroying a possible harmonious relationship with the absent parent (Eph. 4:15).

The age of your children will determine what they are able to hear and bear. In John 16:12 NLT, Jesus said to His disciples, "Oh, there is so much more I want to tell you, but you can't bear it now." Don't overburden your children. Remember Romans 8:1 NKJV: "There is therefore now no condemnation to those who are in Christ Jesus, who do not walk according to the flesh, but according to the Spirit."

Prayer

Lord, in the name of Jesus, I approach Your throne of grace with confidence, so that I may receive mercy and find grace to help my family in our time of need. Father, You are a merciful God; You will not abandon us or destroy us.

In the name of Jesus, I forgive my debtors, including those who have offended, rejected, or abandoned my children and me, or otherwise caused us pain and suffering. Holy Spirit, I call on You to give me the words to explain to my children why their mom/dad does not live with us. I purpose to be honest with my children [speaking truly, dealing truly, and living truly], telling them only that which they can bear, that which is appropriate according to their ages.

Lord, I cry out to You; make haste to me! Give ear to my voice when I cry out to You. Let my prayer be set before You as incense, the lifting up of my hands as the evening sacrifice. Set a guard, O Lord, over my mouth; keep watch over the door of my lips.

Help me to listen with an open heart, recognizing my children's hurt and anger—even their self-blame. Holy Spirit, give me words of comfort when we talk, and help me answer their questions with grace-filled words. Prepare their hearts to hear when I share why we are living alone.

Father, You are a present help in the midst of trouble. You will never leave us or forsake us. I depend on You as my Partner, believing that all things work together and are [fitting into a plan] for good because we love You and are called according to Your design and purpose.

In the name of Jesus. Amen.

Scripture References

Hebrews 4:16 NIV	Psalm 141:1-3 NKJV
Deuteronomy 4:31 NIV	Psalm 46:1
Matthew 6:12 NIV	Hebrews 13:5
Ephesians 4:15 AMP	Romans 8:28 AMP

To Receive Jesus as Your Lord and Savior

Father, it is written in Your Word that if I confess with my mouth that Jesus is Lord and believe in my heart that You have raised Him from the dead, I shall be saved. Therefore, Father, I confess that Jesus is my Lord. I make Him Lord of my life right now. I believe in my heart that You raised Jesus from the dead. I renounce my past life with Satan and close the door to any of his devices.

I thank You for forgiving me of all my sin. Jesus is my Lord, and I am a new creation. Old things have passed away; now all things become new in Jesus' name, amen.

Scripture References

Romans 10:9,10	John 16:8,9
1 John 1:9	Romans 5:8
2 Corinthians 5:17	John 14:6
John 3:16	Romans 10:13
John 6:37	Ephesians 2:1-10
John 10:10	John 1:12
Romans 3:23	2 Corinthians 5:21
2 Corinthians 5:19	

To Be Filled With the Spirit

My heavenly Father, I am Your child, for I believe in my heart that Jesus has been raised from the dead, and I have confessed Him as my Lord.

Jesus said, "How much more shall your heavenly Father give the Holy Spirit to those who ask Him!" (Luke 11:13 NKJV). I ask You now in the name of Jesus to fill me with the Holy Spirit. I step into the fullness and power that I desire in the name of Jesus. I confess that I am a Spirit-filled Christian. As I yield my vocal organs, I expect to speak in tongues, for the Spirit gives me utterance in the name of Jesus. Praise the Lord! Amen.

Scripture References

Romans 10:9,10	Acts 10:44-46
John 14:16,17	Acts 19:2,5,6
Luke 11:13	Romans 10:9,10
Acts 1:8	1 Corinthians 14:2-15
Acts 2:4	1 Corinthians 14:18,27
Acts 2:32,33,39	Ephesians 6:18
Acts 8:12-17	Jude 1:20

About the Author

Germaine Griffin Copeland, founder and president of Word Ministries, Inc., is the author of the *Prayers That Avail Much*® family of books. Her writings provide scriptural prayer instruction to help you pray effectively for those things that concern you and your family and for other prayer assignments. Her teachings on prayer, the personal growth of the intercessor, emotional healing, and related subjects have brought understanding, hope, healing, and liberty to the discouraged and emotionally wounded. She is a woman of prayer and praise whose highest form of worship is the study of God's Word. Her greatest desire is to know God.

Word Ministries, Inc. is a prayer and teaching ministry. Germaine believes that God has called her to teach the practical application of the Word of Truth for successful, victorious living. After years of searching diligently for truth and trying again and again to come out of depression, she decided that she was a mistake. Out of the depths of despair she called upon the name of the Lord, and the light of God's presence invaded the room where she was sitting.

It was in that moment that she experienced the warmth of God's love; old things passed away, and she felt brand new. She discovered a motivation for living—life had purpose. Living in the presence of God, she has found unconditional love and acceptance, healing for crippled emotions, contentment that overcomes depression, peace in the midst of adverse circumstances, and grace for developing healthy relationships. The ongoing process of transformation evolved into praying for others, and the prayer of intercession became her prayer focus.

Germaine is the daughter of the late Reverend A. H. "Buck" and Donnis Brock Griffin. She and her husband, Everette, have four children, and their prayer assignments increase as grandchildren and great-grandchildren are born into the family. Germaine and Everette reside in Roswell, a suburb of Atlanta, Georgia.

MISSION STATEMENT

Word Ministries, Inc.

Motivating individuals to pray
Encouraging them to achieve intimacy with God
Bringing emotional wholeness and spiritual growth

You may contact Word Ministries by writing:

Word Ministries, Inc.
38 Sloan Street • Roswell, Georgia 30075
or calling 770-518-1065

www.prayers.org

*Please include your testimonies
and praise reports when you write.*

OTHER BOOKS BY GERMAINE COPELAND

A Call to Prayer

The Road God Walks

Prayers That Avail Much Commemorative Gift Edition

Prayers That Avail Much Commemorative Leather Edition

Prayers That Avail Much for Business

Prayers That Avail Much Volume 1

Prayers That Avail Much Volume 1—mass market edition

Prayers That Avail Much Volume 2

Prayers That Avail Much Volume 2—mass market edition

Prayers That Avail Much Volume 3

Prayers That Avail Much Volume 3—mass market edition

Prayers That Avail Much for Men

Prayers That Avail Much for Women

Prayers That Avail Much for Mothers—hardbound

Prayers That Avail Much for Mothers—paperback

Prayers That Avail Much for Teens

Prayers That Avail Much for Kids

Prayers That Avail Much for Kids—Book 2

Prayers That Avail Much for the Workplace

Oraciones Con Poder-Prayers That Avail Much (Spanish Edition)

Available from your local bookstore.

THE HARRISON HOUSE VISION

Proclaiming the truth and the power

Of the Gospel of Jesus Christ

With excellence;

Challenging Christians to

Live victoriously,

Grow spiritually,

Know God intimately.